A NEW ISOLATIONISM:
THREAT OR PROMISE?

Other Potomac Associates Books

POTOMAC ASSOCIATES is a nonpartisan research and analysis organization which seeks to encourage lively inquiry into critical issues of public policy. Its purpose is to heighten public understanding and improve public discourse on significant contemporary problems, national and international.

POTOMAC ASSOCIATES provides a forum for distinctive points of view through publication of timely studies and occasional papers by outstanding authorities in the United States and abroad. Although publication implies belief by Potomac Associates in the basic importance and validity of each study, views expressed are those of the author.

POTOMAC ASSOCIATES is a non-tax-exempt firm located at 1707 L Street, NW, Washington, DC 20036.

A Potomac Associates Book

A NEW ISOLATIONISM: THREAT OR PROMISE?

Robert W. Tucker

UNIVERSE BOOKS
New York

Library of Congress Catalog Card Number: 70–189115
ISBN 0–87663–171–5
Design by Hubert Leckie
Printed in the United States of America in 1972 by Universe Books,
381 Park Avenue South, New York, New York 10016
© 1972 by Potomac Associates

CONTENTS

FOREWORD

WITHIN A SURPRISINGLY SHORT PERIOD OF TIME, *discussion and debate on American foreign policy have undergone a marked transformation. The singular concentration on Vietnam, to the exclusion from many forums of almost all other foreign matters, has given way to a far more wide-ranging—and for the body politic far more healthy—deliberation of the fundamentals of our foreign policy and international security position.*

Reasons for this shift are not difficult to find. American involvement in the ground war in Indochina is, to use one of those particularly abhorrent phrases of contemporary official terminology, "winding down." No matter how repugnant to many the continued extensive use of American air and naval power may be, the cold political fact is that troop withdrawals and reduced American combat casualties go a long way toward muting much of the most vocal US opposition to the war.

In addition, the nation and the world have become ever more fascinated with a President who has concentrated his energies heavily in the foreign arena, who has drawn much of the most critical and sensitive policy formulation and implementation into his own direct purview through his hand-picked White House foreign affairs staff, and who has demonstrated a striking flair for the unexpected, frequently leaving friend and foe alike stunned, speechless, and not a little apprehensive.

As much as these developments have widened the scope of foreign policy debate and discussion, their very drama (heightened time and again by dramatic presentation) has had the unfortunate ancillary effect of focussing attention on process instead of substance, on specifics of action rather than underlying assumptions and long-range implications.

In the pages that follow, Robert Tucker looks beyond these surface considerations and asks some fundamental—and refreshingly iconoclastic—questions about the nature of our security interests. In the process he develops a case for a foreign policy based on a far more restricted definition of America's role in the world. A large number of shibboleths need kicking if one is to argue a rational and intelligent case for a new isolationism. Tucker does some lively kicking.

The concept of an isolationist foreign policy, however portrayed and presented, is bound to offend many. This is especially so in the case of Professor Tucker's thesis, since his suggestions, if carried out in literal form, would entail a truly radical reorientation of policy, not the more modest shifts in recent and current trends that underlie much present neo-isolationist thought.

But before such a concept can be dismissed or put aside, the case in its favor must be considered on its own merits, not lightly attacked nor impugned on emotional and subjective grounds. The need for rational and objective debate on so fundamental an issue lends a special importance and timeliness to this book.

In the epilogue, Professor Tucker deals with several objections and alleged omissions raised by critics during various presentations he has made. One or two other themes are worth dealing with here.

What would the political realities of a militarily and diplomatically isolationist foreign policy be? Would the imperative of the ballot box and a two-term presidency tend to rule against a substantially limited American presence in the world? Is, for example, President Nixon's enormously visible and apparently popular venture into summitry typical of what could become a "third-year-of-the-first-term" syndrome, an irresistible itch to take to the global highways as a highly effective way of strengthening re-election prospects? Only time will tell.

And what might the isolationist policy that Professor Tucker outlines look like in the real world? Paradoxically, one might not have to go too far beyond the limits of current developments to imagine a logical scenario consistent with the discussion in the pages that follow.

Vietnamization, after all, represents a distinct and continuing reduction of American military and diplomatic commitment in Southeast Asia. Furthermore, both the SEATO and CENTO treaty involvements, introduced with such fanfare in an earlier era of pactomania, have by now largely atrophied through a tacit policy of simply ignoring them. And what has happened to our commitment to the Alliance for Progress? The fact is, of course, that this administration, disenchanted with the unfulfilled promises and expectations of its predecessors, has sharply curtailed that commitment, in part because foreign policy energies have been concentrated elsewhere.

Finally, may not one ask whether the Nixon Doctrine itself carries within it the unacknowledged seeds of a new isolationism? However politely we tell our friends and allies that their first line of defense must rest with their own capabilities, and that involvement on our part will result in large measure only to the extent that our own security is threatened, is this not a subtle and yet explicit limitation of our global commitment, quite capable of leading to a formally isolationist posture? Indeed, this would not be the first time in history that men have taken policy actions that subsequently pushed them far beyond the limits they initially had in mind.

Many will contend that Professor Tucker could have simplified things for himself by finding a new term for the kind of policy he proposes. Why force controversy by insisting on the use of a term—isolationism—held in such violent contempt by many and historically discredited in the eyes of still more?

In a sense, that is precisely the merit of sticking, with stubborn intellectual persistence and honesty, to the original terminology. By setting the debate in its starkest terms, the author directly challenges those who disagree most sharply to prove him wrong.

William Watts
President, Potomac Associates

PREFACE

IN A NOW CLASSIC CRITIQUE of American foreign policy, Walter Lippmann declared: "For over a century Americans have believed that the undesirability of alliances was so self-evident as to be outside the pale of discussion. Now an objection which men will not examine and debate is a prejudice." * What Lippmann wrote nearly thirty years ago of the American attitude toward alliances may with equal justice be written today of the prevailing attitude toward isolationism. For over a generation, Americans have believed that the undesirability of isolationism was so self-evident as to be outside the pale of discussion. No less than an earlier objection to alliances, the contemporary objection to isolationism is a prejudice. It may be an understandable prejudice, in view of US experience between World War I and World War II, but it is a prejudice nonetheless.

So marked is this prejudice that in the American political vocabulary there are few terms carrying greater opprobrium than isolationism. Although men may no longer know what isolationism means, they do know it is

---

* Walter Lippmann, *U.S. Foreign Policy: Shield of the Republic* (Boston: Little, Brown & Co., 1943), p. 58.

a label to be avoided. There is something absurd in this tyranny and in the nonsensical exchanges to which it has given rise.

Isolationism is not to be identified with "quitting the world," something we have never done and will never do. It is not to be identified with the absence of all significant relationships but, rather, with the absence of certain relationships. As a policy, isolationism is above all generally characterized by the refusal to enter into alliances and to undertake military interventions. This was the essential meaning of an isolationist policy in the past, and it remains the essential meaning of an isolationist policy today.

When is an isolationist policy possible or desirable? The answer to this question cannot be determined independently of time and circumstance. The conviction that it can characterized the isolationists of yesterday. That same conviction characterizes those today who simply dismiss the possibility of a new isolationism.

In this essay, I argue that a new isolationism for the United States is quite possible in the sense that it could be undertaken without sacrifice of or jeopardy to physical security, material well-being, or the integrity of our institutions. The contrary view is rooted in an analysis of the international environment and of US security requirements that was once valid but is no longer so. A new isolationism would surely require time in order to effect the considerable changes involved. Given a decade, however, the requisite changes could be made. Most of them could be consummated in an even shorter period.

Although isolationism is possible, it may still be argued that its effects would prove undesirable. On examination, though, the grim prospects often drawn of the hostile world presumably attending an isolationist America appear quite unrealistic. Even so, it is by no means unrealistic to expect that a new isolationism would be attended by a marked decline in US influence. An isolationist America would not be an isolated America, but it would of course be an America that has given up the preponderant role it has played since World War II.

It would be a signal error to believe that the aspirations marking American foreign policy for so long might be easily relinquished, however. Nations, like individuals, must suffer a great deal before they are ready to abandon the vision—or illusion—they entertain of themselves. Certainly there is reason to doubt that the foreign policy elites have changed fundamentally in outlook, and this despite the sobering experience of Vietnam. There is also reason to doubt that the public will impose novel constraints on the executive's future freedom of action, and this despite the present ambivalence in the public's mood.

For these and yet other reasons, this essay ends on a note of uncertainty over the future of US foreign policy. The circumstances that were ultimately decisive in leading the nation to abandon its interwar isolationism have changed, and radically so. It does not follow, however, that the role and interests resulting from the circumstances of yesterday will now change to reflect the altered circumstances of today. Even if they do not, there is value in pointing out the extent to which America's present role and interests are the result of a concept of security that can no longer account for this role and these interests. The purpose of this inquiry is not to show that the emperor has no clothes. It is instead to show that the garment the emperor is wearing is different from that he has pretended to wear and many still believe they have seen.

I FEARS OF A NEW ISOLATIONISM

IS THERE A SERIOUS PROSPECT that America will revert to
an isolationist posture in the wake of the Vietnam War?

Two administrations have now expressed the fear that
the nation may yet abandon its present role and interests
in the world. Almost from the outset of the debate engendered by Vietnam, President Lyndon B. Johnson and his
secretary of state, Dean Rusk, insistently compared oppo-
nents of the war, however liberal and moderate, with the
isolationists of the 1930s. President Richard M. Nixon has
persisted in this comparison with his vision of an elite
that has turned its back on "internationalism." "The irony
today, for those who look at the Washington scene," Nixon
observed in an interview with *New York Times* columnist
C. L. Sulzberger, "is that the great internationalists of the
post-World War II period have become the neo-isolationists
of the Vietnam War period and especially of the period
accompanying the ending of the war."* It is those who
formed the core of the post-World War II consensus on foreign policy, in the President's term, "the Establishment,"
who have presumably broken the internationalist faith of
a generation. It is "the people who, after World War II,

---

* *New York Times*, March 10, 1971, p. 14.

supported the Greek-Turkish aid program, the Marshall Plan, NATO" who are today in "disarray" because of Vietnam and a one-sided concern for domestic problems.

Nor is it only the presumed defection of the Establishment that has aroused presidential concern over the threat of a new isolationism. In the interview cited above, President Nixon expressed less than complete faith in the general public's understanding and support of America's global role and responsibilities. Although conceding that he had "far more confidence in our people than in the Establishment . . . to do the right thing," the President was nevertheless certain that a Gallup poll would show that a great majority of people "would want to pull out of Vietnam . . . pull three or more divisions out of Europe and . . . cut our defense budget." For this reason, he concluded: "Polls are not the answer. You must look at the facts."

There is no reason to question the President's assessment of what a public opinion poll would show. Recent opinion surveys do indeed indicate that a majority of the public presently favors a restricted US world role. They also indicate that a majority views with disfavor the future use of American troops abroad, even to defend allied states against overt communist aggression.* The question remains, of course, whether these public preferences indicate a serious turn to isolationism or register little more than a passing mood responsive to the US experience in Vietnam. Even if they do reveal an outlook that may be expected to persist in the years following our involvement in Vietnam, there is the further question of whether it is misleading to characterize this outlook as one of isolationism.

---

* Albert H. Cantril and Charles W. Roll, *Hopes and Fears of the American People* (New York: Universe Books, 1971), p. 45.

What are we to make of presidential fears of a revival of isolationism? Has the President confused opposition to his policy in Vietnam with isolationism? Has he misread the nature of the more general criticism made of American foreign policy?

That the President has done so is clearly the view taken by many of his articulate critics. The charge of isolationism, they claim, is little more than a rhetorical diversion that serves to obfuscate the real issues. The immediate issue is how to end a war that has proven disastrous to American well-being at home and to the nation's enduring interests abroad. Beyond Vietnam, the issue is not one of withdrawal from the world but one of redefining America's relationship to the world. To equate such a redefinition with neo-isolationism, the critics claim, reflects either an inability or an unwillingness to distinguish between America's general involvement in the world and the precise nature and extent of this involvement.

The response to presidential fears of neo-isolationism goes beyond the contention that the President has confused neo-isolationism with something that is, in reality, very different. On a more detached level of analysis, a number of observers have sought to show that the changes, domestic and foreign, that have occurred since World War II preclude a return to isolationism.

Thus, it has been pointed out that America's interwar isolationism rested in large part on a rural and ethnic base. Whereas a rural America persisted in the belief that the nation could insulate itself from events abroad, an ethnic America evoked opposition to intervention in Europe on the part of groups motivated by pro-German and anti-British bias (since intervention in Europe meant, in practice, intervention on behalf of Great Britain against

Germany). In the changed circumstances of the period following World War II, this parochial and ethnic base of interwar isolationism was all but destroyed. With the emergence of the Soviet Union (and, more generally, communism) as the great protagonist, the *raison d'etre* of ethnic isolationism disappeared. With the urbanization of America and the emergence of a better educated and more widely traveled society with a pervasive sense of world involvement, the xenophobia that formed an important ingredient in the traditional isolationist outlook has also largely disappeared.

If changes in culture and communications have presumably destroyed the intellectual and emotional underpinnings of interwar isolationism as an outlook, economic and strategic realities are considered to preclude the possibility of a return to isolationism as a policy. Our economic commitment abroad, it is argued, compels a course of action that rules out a return to isolationism. Economic interdependence is for the United States an inescapable fact of life, and one that may be disregarded only at the price of national well-being.

Even more important is the interdependence that is held to result from the existence of nuclear weapons. The problems these weapons create are soluble, if at all, only through international action. The threat to US security arising from nuclear proliferation, it is argued, compels this nation to pursue a policy incompatible with isolationism. For proliferation, and particularly the kind of proliferation likely to follow a general American withdrawal from alliance commitments, would appreciably increase the danger of nuclear war, a danger that America could not reasonably expect to avoid.

Finally, there is the argument that the very magnitude

of America's power precludes a return to isolationism. Although there are many variations of this familiar theme, its common denominator may be found in the proposition that power creates responsibilities. Men may and do differ over the nature of these responsibilities, just as they may and do differ over the means by which these responsibilities are to be carried out. Even so, their disagreements do not affect the shared belief that great power must in turn give rise to great responsibility, and that this responsibility is incompatible with isolationism. A persistent supporter of an imperial America, apprehensive over the isolationism he finds among the nation's intellectuals, writes that "a great power does not have the freedom of action—derived from the freedom of inaction—that a small power possesses. It is entangled in a web of responsibilities from which there is no hope of escape.* A persistent critic of an imperial America, in dismissing the possibility that we might ignore our responsibilities to the world, declares: "With the world's most powerful economy and mightiest military force, the United States could never again be isolationist." **

---

* Irving Kristol, "American Intellectuals and Foreign Policy," *Foreign Affairs*, July 1967, p. 602.

** Ronald Steel, *Imperialists and Other Heroes: The Imperial Generation and the End of the American Dream* (New York: Random House, 1971), p. 428–29.

II THE MEANING OF ISOLATIONISM

WHATEVER THE MERIT OF THE ARGUMENTS against a new isolationism, it is difficult to assess them in the absence of a reasonably clear view of what isolationism meant in the past and what it might mean today. Whether or not a new isolationism is possible and, if possible, desirable depends in large measure on the meaning given to isolationism—and, by implication, to its apparent opposite, internationalism.*

At the very least, the meaning of isolationism cannot simply be a matter of self-perception among the critics of US foreign policy. If it were, the prospects of a new isolationism clearly would be non-existent. On one point, at least, there is agreement among almost all of them. By self-definition, nearly all are internationalist, or, at any rate, anti-isolationist.

Thus, it is not only the moderate critics of US foreign policy—those comprising the bulk of President Nixon's

---

* "Apparent opposite," since some forms of "internationalism" may prove indistinguishable in practice from isolationism. It is a further gloss on the terminological difficulties attending debates over US foreign policy that in an earlier period "internationalism" was equated with "interventionism." In the 1930s and 1940s, one was an internationalist only by being an interventionist.

Establishment—who dismiss the charge that they have become the new isolationists. The charge is rejected by those who call for more fundamental policy departures as well. In a recent speech, the chairman of the Senate Committee on Foreign Relations, Senator J. William Fulbright, urged the reconsideration of "our most basic assumptions about international relations." It is not enough, he declared, simply to question America's present role and interests in the world; we must go further and question the very premises on which the entire game of "power politics" has heretofore been conducted. In calling for such reconsiderations, Senator Fulbright does not think of himself as a lapsed internationalist. On the contrary, he considers himself a true believer. What is necessary, he insists, is to distinguish between the new internationalism and the old. "People who are now being called 'neo-isolationists' are by and large those who make a distinction between the new internationalism and the old, who regret the reversion to the old power politics, and who retain some faith in the validity and vitality of the United Nations idea."*

It is the old internationalism, then, the internationalism of the cold war, with its alliances, competition in arms, and interventions, that Senator Fulbright rejects. A similar theme appears in much of the criticism made of US foreign policy by articulate members of the younger generation. To the degree that they are willing to identify themselves as isolationists, they are so only with respect to the "old diplomacy" of the cold war. With respect to the "new diplomacy," however, which is presumably concerned with "real people and their needs," they are anything but isolationists. This view suggests how one of them can write,

---

* *Congressional Record*, Ninety-second Congress, First Session, April 14, 1971, p. S4787.

with no intended irony, that "a new internationalism based on a peaceful response to human needs is the only effective response that the new generation of isolationists will heed." *

Even the apparent isolationism of the group most hostile to American foreign policy, the radical left, turns out to be something less than pure. It is true that in the radical critique there is an unqualified rejection of America's present role and interests in the world. Yet, if the radical demand that the empire be dismantled as seen as a demand for America's isolation, it remains the case that the isolationism of the radical left is still a provisional isolationism. It is only a capitalist America that is a repressive force in the world and that must be isolated within it. With the advent of socialism, however, the reason for America's isolation would disappear, for a socialist America would presumably be a liberating force in the world. The radical is only an isolationist for the present. For the future—a future in which a sinful nation may yet redeem itself—he is a complete internationalist.**

Nor does the general public see itself as isolationist. Since World War II it has been axiomatic that, when asked about the desirability of the United States's participating in world affairs and working closely with other nations, a large majority of the public has responded affirmatively. Despite the Vietnam War, this response persists substantially unchanged. Whatever the shifts in public attitudes on more specific issues of military and foreign

---

* James A. Johnson, "The New Generation of Isolationists," *Foreign Affairs*, October 1970, p. 146.

** See Robert W. Tucker, *The Radical Left and American Foreign Policy* (Baltimore: The Johns Hopkins Press, 1971).

policy, the public's general image of itself as internationalist is clear.*

If the prospects of a new isolationism cannot rest simply on the self-perceptions of citizens, critics, and policymakers, neither can the prospects be usefully assessed in terms of the literal meaning of isolationism. It is absurd to ask where are the isolationists today, if by isolationism we mean the absence of any significant relationships between America and the rest of the world. A small minority apart, no one seriously advocates either the possibility or the desirability of a genuinely isolated America. Nor, for that matter, do those who profess to fear a revival of isolationism seriously argue that isolationism would mean the absence of all significant relationships between America and the other nations of the world. What they do argue is that a new isolationism, were it to prevail, would be characterized by the refusal to maintain certain relationships, to undertake certain actions, and that this refusal would in turn eventually jeopardize interests that even neo-isolationists would have to acknowledge as vital.

Isolationism, in the literal sense, is not only irrelevant in the contemporary context; it is also largely irrelevant when applied to the nation's past. America has never pursued a policy of genuine isolation.

From the beginning of the nation's history, isolationism has been given neither commercial nor consistent ideological expression. US commerce and trade with the world have

---

* In response to the Gallup poll trend question, "Would it be better for the United States to keep independent in world affairs—or would it be better for the United States to work closely with other nations?" public support for working closely with other nations was 78 percent in 1953, 82 percent in 1963, 79 percent in 1967, and 72 percent in January 1969. The practical significance of this question, and questions of a similar nature, is discussed in chapter VI.

grown concomitantly with the growth of the nation. A policy of economic self-sufficiency has never been seriously considered. Instead, belief in the desirability and, indeed, the necessity of US foreign economic expansion has been taken largely for granted since well before the turn of the century. This belief, moreover, has commonly gone hand in hand with a commitment, however general, to ideological expansion. Isolationists have supported the American mission of bringing the blessings of freedom to all men (and not only Americans), though they have insisted that this purpose be achieved through a policy of political non-entanglement. Accordingly, the American purpose encompassed from the start the idea of a national duty, a duty to be implemented through the power of example.

The classic expression of America's historic policy of isolation is to be found, as everyone knows, in Washington's Farewell Address of 1796. "The great rule of conduct for us in regard to foreign nations," Washington declared, "is, in extending our commercial relations to have with them as little political connection as possible. . . . Europe has a set of primary interests which to us have none or a very remote relation. Hence she must be engaged in frequent controversies, the causes of which are essentially foreign to our concerns. Hence, therefore, it must be unwise in us to implicate ourselves by artificial ties in the ordinary vicissitudes of her politics or the ordinary combinations and collisions of her friendships or enmities. Our detached and distant situation invites and enables us to pursue a different course." The different course Washington advised was "to steer clear of permanent alliances with any portion of the foreign world, so far . . . as we are now at liberty to do it" and to "safely trust to temporary alliances for extraordinary emergencies."

Washington's advice was cast in qualified and tentative terms. The "great rule of conduct" urged upon the nation was not set forth as an absolute principle that represented, whatever the circumstances, the enduring interests of the nation, but as a policy for consolidating a newly won independence and a still precarious security. At the time it was given, it represented more an aspiration than a reality. So long as the new American state did not enjoy security of its frontiers, so long as it was not free from the danger of interference with the development of the West, above all, so long as it had not secured possession of the Mississippi Valley, it could not disavow the prospect of an alliance, even a permanent alliance, with a European power. The policy of isolation or non-entanglement could, and did, become a reality only with the territorial expansion occurring in the first two decades of the nineteenth century. The Monroe Doctrine, which came at the close of this first great period of expansion, reiterated Washington's "great rule of conduct" and, in proclaiming the separation of the "two spheres," sought to give the policy of hemispheric isolation significance.

It is important to recall that in the American experience an isolationist policy has not precluded an expansionist policy. Although the view persists that isolation and expansion cannot be reconciled, it is evidently the case that the nation did pursue both courses throughout most of the nineteenth century. A policy of territorial expansion over the continent had as one of its principal justifications the end of ensuring political isolation from Europe. That same end also provided one of the principal justifications for America's policy of expansion in the hemisphere. In the policy of the "two spheres," America's intended hegemony in the New World was to serve as the necessary means for guaranteeing hemispheric political isolation.

In the period following the turn of the century, isolationism was no longer given even consistent political expression outside the Western Hemisphere. Through acquisition of the Philippines and a commitment, however qualified, to the Open Door in China, America became a party to the politics of East Asia.

World War I, and the decisive part American intervention played, led to far more significant departures from the position the nation had occupied in the nineteenth century. Though refusing to be a party to the postwar settlement in Europe, America played a critical role in defining the nature of that settlement by virtue of her intervention in the war and her participation in the peace conference that followed. In the Pacific and Asia, too, America assumed a dominant role in defining the postwar settlement and was a party to it.

The period between World War I and World War II can scarcely be characterized as one in which the United States occupied a position of literal isolation. On the contrary, the years between the wars were marked by the steady, if unspectacular, expansion of American influence and interests, particularly economic interests. In turn, this expansion, with its evident bias in favor of stability and the *status quo*, was supported, though with varying effectiveness, by America's increasing economic power.

Given the growth of US interests, a revisionist historiography has concluded that the nation's interwar isolationism is a myth designed to obscure the essential continuity of an expansionist policy pursued throughout this century, and not only in the period following World War II.* But this

---

* See William A. Williams, *The Tragedy of American Diplomacy*, rev. ed. (New York: Dell Publishing Co., 1962).

argument largely rests upon the confusion of aspiration with policy. Even granting revisionist contentions that the aspiration of policy-makers in the interwar years was to achieve a stable liberal-capitalist world order under American leadership, the point remains that American diplomacy was characterized throughout by an unwillingness to adopt the means necessary to realize this aspiration. What isolationism as a policy signified in this period was nothing more nor less than the refusal to guarantee the post-World War I *status quo* in Europe and Asia against change by force of arms. The issue of America's isolationism cannot be determined primarily by examining the growth of the nation's interests and the scope of its aspirations. It must also take into account what measures America has been prepared to take to preserve those interests and to realize those aspirations, however they are defined.

The prospects of a new isolationism cannot be dismissed then, by showing the implausibility (if not the impossibility) of an America that no longer plays any role and that no longer retains any interests in the world. America has never adopted such a policy, and it is altogether unlikely that she ever will. Nor can these prospects be dismissed by showing the implausibility of a new isolationism that would duplicate the old. In a number of respects, a new isolationism, were it to materialize, would not resemble the isolationism of the past. Thus, a new isolationism would not be characterized by the parochialism and suspicion of all things foreign that marked so much of the old isolationism. (Though not all of the old. There was a liberal-left strain in the old isolationism that was in no sense xenophobic. On the contrary, in their own way, these isolationists were quite as "internationalist" as the "new generation of isolationists.")

Nor is it likely that a new isolationism would follow the old in making unilateralism the touchstone of policy. It is this traditional emphasis on unilateralism, this insistence on retaining America's complete freedom of action, that in part explains the otherwise mysterious disparity in isolationist attitudes toward involvement in Europe and in Asia. Whereas America's intervention in Europe necessarily implied entangling relationships with nations that would be roughly our equals (Great Britain and France), intervention in Asia was based on the assumption that such relationships could be avoided, since our putative adversary (Japan) was the only major power in the region. Accordingly, it was in Asia that some isolationists were willing to engage the nation's interests and power, while refusing to do so in Europe. As late as the period of the Korean War, this disposition was expressed in the isolationist resurgence among right-wing Republicans. It was in Asia that the then "new isolationists" pushed for a more aggressive foreign policy and sought to concentrate American efforts. At the same time, it was in Asia that we were urged, in the expression of the day, "to go it alone." *

---

* It would be misleading to suggest, however, that unilateralism is a trait that has characterized isolationists alone. Given the nature of the American diplomatic experience, a disposition to unilateralism was an expected consequence. Nor did the nation abandon this disposition when it abandoned its aversion to territorial commitments outside the Western Hemisphere. In the period following World War II, America's vast power and the weakness of her allies meant that her commitments were for all practical purposes unilateral in character. And in Asia, despite the vast changes that have occurred in the past generation, a unilateralist policy, in substance if not in form, has persisted to this day. It has marked America's intervention in Vietnam.

In large measure, then, America's postwar devotion to forms of multilateralism has masked the substance of unilateral action. For the very strong, multilateralism is at once a luxury, in that it does not materially restrict their behavior, and an advantage, in that it gives their actions a legitimacy they might otherwise not possess.

There is no indication today that a new isolationism would either reflect the same disparity toward Europe and Asia that the old isolationism reflected, or support a policy of unilateral intervention in Asia. On the contrary, should a new isolationism materialize, there is every reason to believe that it would be applied in Asia. To the extent that a disparity is drawn between Europe and Asia by those presumably attracted to a new isolationism, the disparity is the reverse of that made by many of the old isolationists. It is above all in Asia that many contemporary critics have sought to disengage US power. And it is above all in Asia that most of them have insisted that if US interests should ever require future military intervention, the *sine qua non* of such intervention must be its genuinely multilateral character.

In still other respects, an older isolationism is unlikely to reappear. The interwar isolationists acknowledged no duty to the world beyond that of serving as a moral example. If the belief has waned that America is capable of setting an example to the world, the conviction persists that America's responsibilities to the world are not exhausted by the example she may be capable—or incapable—of setting. In relation to the poor nations, there is the general recognition that America has an obligation to assist in their development. (It is another matter to ask how seriously this obligation would be taken in practice by an America that no longer believed its fate to be substantially tied to the fate of the developing states.) In relation to all nations, there is an awareness of a responsibility implicit in the possession of the destructive power conferred by nuclear weapons.

As recent events indicate, however, the multilateral obsession may be expected to diminish as America's power to enjoin others to do her bidding diminishes.

Moreover, it is the common currency of most critics to in-sist that these duties can only be satisfactorily carried out through means that are the antithesis of the absolute inde-pendence of action so fervently held to by an older isola-tionism.

The point need not be labored. A new isolationism, were it to materialize, would be new, at least in some respects. It does not follow that a new isolationism is impossible, unless of course it is assumed that we must have either the old isolationism or none at all. Yet it is precisely this as-sumption that underlies so much current discussion of neo-isolationism. The prospects of a new isolationism, it is com-monly assumed, must be equated with the prospects of resurrecting the isolationism of the interwar period. And since it is apparent that we are not going to have the old isolationism, that the old isolationism cannot be resur-rected, if only because America and the world of the 1970s are very different from America and the world of the 1920s and 1930s, it is concluded that we shall have no isolation-ism at all.

That isolationism is equated today with the interwar experience is scarcely surprising. Nor is it surprising, in the light of this experience, that the charge of isolationism is almost invariably rejected by those against whom it is made. For the interwar experience signifies to most of us an outlook and policy that persistently neglected, and ulti-mately imperiled through this neglect, the nation's vital interests. The prevailing judgment of America's interwar isolationism is that it led us to a point of near-disaster by virtue of its inability to appreciate the nation's vital inter-ests and its unwillingness to employ the means necessary to vindicate those interests.

At issue here is not the prevailing judgment of America's

interwar isolationism but the insistence on applying this judgment to a new isolationism. Whether a new isolationism must call forth a similar judgment cannot be decided in the abstract, for the folly or wisdom—the threat or the promise—of isolationism cannot be decided in the abstract. In its classic and enduring usage, isolationism has an entirely neutral meaning. (It also has a relative meaning, in that a state may pursue an isolationist policy toward some regions and not toward others.) As a policy, isolationism signifies the refusal to entertain certain relationships, notably alliances, and to undertake certain actions, notably interventions. As a status, isolation has been occasionally sought after and more often feared, depending upon circumstance and interest.

During most of the nineteenth century, circumstance permitted the United States to pursue an isolationist policy toward the world beyond the Western Hemisphere. That policy, it is generally agreed, corresponded with the nation's interests. If a very different judgment is made of America's interwar isolationist policy, it is not only because the circumstances of the American position had changed but also because America's interests had changed. In the twentieth century, and particularly in the interwar period, circumstance and interest combined to turn what was once deemed a prudent and desirable policy into an imprudent and undesirable one. But from this judgment, it does not follow that the prospects of a new isolationism may be ruled out nor that a new isolationism would of necessity neglect, and even threaten, the nation's vital interests.

Thus, to raise the issue of neo-isolationism is to raise in their most pointed form the central issues of American foreign policy today. To ask whether a new isolationism is possible is to ask whether the domestic and international

environment make it possible. To ask whether a new isolationism is desirable is to ask whether American interests
would be better served by a withdrawal from postwar
commitments and an avoidance of new ones.

Whatever the answers to these questions, they cannot
simply be dismissed by arguing that a new isolationism is
precluded because a number of elements sustaining the old
isolationism have disappeared. A new isolationism may
rest upon a different domestic base than did the old. It is
not only an insular and parochial America that may sustain
an isolationist outlook, just as it is not only an ethnic
America that may oppose intervention even in Europe. Indeed, it would be a mistake to assume that these factors
provided the principal support for America's interwar isolationism. The belief in unilateralism, the insistence upon
retaining complete independence of action, cannot be attributed primarily to insularity, education, or ethnic origin.
Nor can the belief that the Western Hemisphere was impregnable and that the greatest threat to America's security
and well-being would result from our involvement in a
foreign war. Yet it was a combination of these two beliefs
that formed the essential base of the old isolationism.

That a new isolationism would not duplicate the old
cannot be taken to mean that there would be no parallels
between the two. On the contrary, it is clear that a number
of beliefs sustaining the old isolationism once again enjoy,
though in varying forms, considerable vogue.

One apparent parallel between yesterday and today is the
belief that American power can make no significant contribution to the solution of the world's problems. In the
1930s this belief was held primarily in relation to Europe;
today it is held primarily in relation to the nations of the
Third World. In the 1930s the isolationist conviction of

America's powerlessness was in large part the result of a negative estimate made of other countries, particularly the European nations; today it is no longer the presumed moral turpitude of others that primarily accounts for the skepticism toward America's efforts in the world. To some, this skepticism is the result of a negative estimate of America. If America is considered powerless, it is so in the sense that there is no longer a belief in the American potential for good. To others, the skepticism results from the conviction that a pluralistic world has become increasingly resistant to American power and purposes. To still others, the skepticism comes from the belief that in the future America will have to expend all her energies on attempting to solve her problems at home. What an America cannot as yet do for itself, it surely cannot do for others. If these groups start from quite different assumptions about the nature and sources of America's powerlessness, they may nevertheless arrive at a common conclusion—and one that points in the direction of a new isolationism.

A more significant parallel than the growing conviction of America's incapacity to change matters in the world for the better (or, at least, to do so through her present policies) is the belief that our global involvement has reached the point at which it directly threatens the nation's political institutions and general well-being.

A concern over the domestic consequences of foreign policy does not, as such, distinguish an isolationist outlook. The insistence that it does is indicative of the extent to which a long generation of cold war and the exercise of imperial power have created a presumption that invariably places the "needs" of foreign policy over those of domestic policy. That presumption, by considering domestic policy as little more than a function of foreign policy, is clearly at variance with a tradition that considers foreign policy as no more than a means to the end of protecting and promoting individual freedom and collective well-being. If there is a point at which foreign policy has primacy over domestic policy, it is only because the security and independence of the state remain the indispensable means to the protection and promotion of individual and societal values. In this traditional view, the ultimate justification of foreign policy must be its contribution to domestic happiness and welfare.

What distinguishes an isolationist outlook, then, is not the insistence that foreign policy be justified in terms of its domestic consequences. It is instead the conviction that sustained foreign involvement—and particularly one holding out the constant prospect of military intervention—poses a grave threat to America's institutions and well-being. An extreme sensitivity to, and consequently an obsessive fear of, the domestic effects of foreign policy has been one of the hallmarks—perhaps *the* hallmark—of the isolationist outlook. Isolationists have of course entertained widely divergent visions of the American promise. What has united them, however, has been their shared belief that foreign involvement—and above all war—erodes constitutional processes and betrays the American promise. In the 1930s it was this belief that united such otherwise disparate figures as Norman Thomas and Senator Robert A. Taft. To Thomas, a socialist and pacifist, American intervention against fascism meant the abandonment of any hope for the nation's economic reorganization. To Taft, a conservative Republican, a war to preserve democracy elsewhere meant the destruction of democracy in the United States and the creation of a socialist dictatorship. Although the context has altered markedly, it is nevertheless essentially the same belief that today prompts Senator Fulbright to declare: "I used to puzzle over the question of how American democracy could be adapted to the kind of role we have come to play in the world. I think I now know the answer: it cannot be done." *

A sense of America's powerlessness to change matters for the better joined with a conviction that pervasive military involvement abroad threatens, directly or indirectly, domestic well-being could form the basis for a substantial American withdrawal from present commitments. This outcome is especially possible to the extent that these trends are accompanied by a changed perception of the nation's vital interests and of what might threaten those interests. The outlook attending a new isolationism need not duplicate that of the old in assuming that America's security cannot be seriously threatened by events occurring beyond this hemisphere. But even falling short of that assumption, which for a time gave coherence and persuasiveness to the old isolationism, such a changed outlook still might alter, and considerably so, the expansive conception of America's security interests that has dominated American policy for almost three decades. By so doing, it would place in serious question the principal and compelling incentive to maintaining America's present role and interests in the world. And, if this outlook were to persist and deepen, it could form the basis for an American withdrawal from postwar commitments.

A new isolationism might well develop under the banner of a new internationalism. However it is termed, it would still be isolationist if characterized by the refusal to entertain certain relationships and to undertake certain actions. This is only to say that the issue of isolationism continues

* *Congressional Record*, Ninety-second Congress, First Session, April 14, 1971, p. S4785.

principally to turn, as it has always turned, on the willingness to enter into—or, in the present context, to retain—military commitments. An anti-interventionist position in principle continues to imply substantially what it implied in the past. Although anti-interventionism may be termed a new internationalism, it will also be a new isolationism.

III THE POSSIBILITY OF A NEW ISOLATIONISM: STRATEGIC REALITIES AND ECONOMIC NECESSITIES

CAN THE UNITED STATES pursue a new isolationism without jeopardy to or sacrifice of vital interests?

The prevailing view, as previously noted, is to consider a negative response almost self-evident. But, to the extent that vital interests are equated with the nation's security, and particularly with its physical security, the persuasiveness of this view is no longer apparent. Instead, what is, or should be, apparent is that a radical change has occurred in the structure of American security in the years since World War II. In consequence, what was once a meaningful prospect to fear and to prepare against through alliances and, when necessary, military intervention is no longer so. The view that strategic realities preclude a new isolationism rests largely upon an analysis of the nation's security requirements that was formed more than a generation ago in circumstances that bear only a remote resemblance to those of the present.

STRATEGIC REALITIES
In the 1930s it was altogether possible to imagine an imbalance of military power that would threaten the physical

security of the Western Hemisphere and, ultimately, of
the United States itself. A hostile power in control of
Europe—even more, a combination of hostile powers in
control of Eurasia—would possess a potential military
strength superior to that of the New World. In these circumstances, it was entirely plausible to argue that America
would become a beleaguered fortress, required to expend
all of her energies in defense of the hemisphere. Even if a
successful hemispheric defense were to prove possible, the
critics of isolationism contended, the result would almost
certainly impose the most severe of strains on the nation's
resources and, in the process, endanger its free institutions.

In analyzing America's interwar policy, Walter Lippmann gave perhaps the most convincing expression to this
view of the American security position and concluded that
isolation "is the worst of all possible predicaments." * In a
balance-of-power system, security ideally consists in being
a member of a combination that is so strong it will not be
challenged. At the very least, the logic of such a system requires allies sufficiently dependable and powerful to meet
and defeat a challenge should it arise.

Isolationists, Lippmann contended, remained blind to
these fundamental truths by virtue of their conviction that
the nation's security was unconditioned by events occurring beyond the Western Hemisphere. Misreading our
nineteenth century experience, they did not see that the
security of this hemisphere had always depended upon a
favorable balance of power in Europe, that is, a balance that
would leave Great Britain in unchallenged command of the
approaches to the Americas. In consequence, they did not
see that the Monroe Doctrine had been conditioned

---

* Lippmann, *U.S. Foreign Policy*, p. 105.

throughout by the assumption that Great Britain would provide primary strategic defense of the hemisphere by restraining other trans-oceanic powers.* Finally, by ignoring the impact of the means of modern warfare on America's strategic requirements, isolationists persisted in their belief that America's security was unconditioned at a time when these means had extended America's strategic defenses "across both oceans and to all the trans-oceanic lands from which an attack by sea or by air can be launched." **

Whatever the merits of Lippmann's interpretation of the past, his analysis of the American position came to enjoy widespread acceptance. It did so, however, only after events had put the isolationist position to the test and it was found wanting. The sudden decline and collapse of interwar isolationism came when the progress of the war appeared to hold out the distinct prospect of an Axis victory, hence the prospect of an America alone in a hostile world. In such a world, America would be permanently confined to a defensive role in the Western Hemisphere. Moreover, once the prospect of a Europe—and, even more, a Eurasia—controlled by hostile powers emerged as a very real one, it was far from certain that the defense of the Western Hemisphere could be successfully undertaken—at least, without

---

* If it is the case that the Monroe Doctrine rested, though only partly so, on British sea-power, it is also the case that Great Britain afforded the only serious challenge to American hegemony in this hemisphere. That this threat stopped short of taking a military form may be explained, in part, by the vulnerability of Canada to American invasion. For the most part, though, British restraint may be attributed simply to the disparity of interest in the several disputes arising between the two states, a disparity that normally favored America.

** "American security at sea has always . . . extended to the coast line of Europe, Africa, and Asia. In the new age of air power it extends beyond the coast line to the lands where there are airdromes from which planes can take off." Lippmann, *U.S. Foreign Policy*, p. 94.

the kind of effort that might eventually imperil prosperity and democracy in America itself.*

To prevent this prospect from materializing, to forestall an imbalance of power that, it was feared, would sooner or later directly threaten the nation's security, the decision was made to adopt a policy that eventually led to forcible intervention. In the end, that decision came to be supported by all but a hard core of isolationists. For the majority of isolationists—let alone the majority of Americans—had not in fact believed that, whatever the course of the war, America's security would remain unconditioned and the Western Hemisphere impregnable. Instead, they had believed that the Axis powers would not be victorious. When this belief was challenged by events, when the nerve roots of the American security position were finally exposed, the isolationists, too, reluctantly moved from non-entanglement to alliance and intervention.

Substantially the same considerations that impelled America's intervention in World War II subsequently led to a course of action that made the cold war inevitable. The postwar consensus on the need to contain communism

---

* It should be recalled that at the height of the mobilization brought on by World War II, America had some 14 million men under arms out of a population of 130 million and was devoting approximately 50 percent of her total resources to the war effort. The fear that a sustained effort of this magnitude would prove incompatible with democratic institutions was not an unreasonable one. In addition, many doubted, with Lippmann, whether a permanently mobilized America could defend the hemisphere. A prominent strategist, Nicholas Spykman, in analyzing the American position, concluded: "The defeat of our allies in the Old World would not permit us to withdraw to a position of hemisphere defense. We would be obliged to surrender the outer belts of the North and South American Buffer Zone and forced to make a last stand in terms of quarter sphere defense in the North American Continental Zone and the American Mediterranean." Nicholas Spykman, *America's Strategy in World Politics* (New York: Harcourt, Brace, 1942), p. 445.

emerged from what was commonly perceived at the time as a direct and serious threat to American security arising from a weak and unstable Western Europe over which the Soviet Union might eventually extend its control. The initial measures of containment, the Marshall Plan and the North Atlantic Alliance, formally expressed (and thereby made unmistakable) the vital American interest in preserving the security and independence of the nations of Western Europe. In the context of Soviet-American rivalry, NATO and the Marshall Plan constituted clear acknowledgment that Russian domination of Western Europe might shift the world balance of power decisively against the United States and thus in time create a threat to America's physical security. At the very least, it was assumed that a Russian-dominated Europe would create a security problem for the United States, the solution of which would strain the nation's resources and jeopardize its institutions.

Given the preponderance of power America enjoyed in the years following the war, it is not surprising that, with hindsight, a conventional security motive as an explanation of early containment policy now appears to many to lack the ring of plausibility. Indeed, a case can be made that by the late 1940s the structure and bases of world power had changed in ways that made the security of America much less dependent upon a European balance of power than was the case only a decade before. But even if postwar security apprehensions were exaggerated—whether from a misreading of Soviet intentions or from a failure to appreciate the extent to which the American position had changed in scarcely a decade—they were not unreasonable.

For America of the middle to late 1940s, the most relevant international experience occurred in the period before and during World War II. This experience included not only the threat held out by a victory of the Axis powers, but also, during 1939-41, the prospect of a Eurasia partitioned and jointly controlled by Germany, Russia, and Japan. Even to a preponderant America, apprehension over a revival of that prospect, though with the Soviet Union as its sole architect and director, was not unreasonable.

Neither US intervention in World War II nor the subsequent pursuit of containment was undertaken solely for reasons of physical security, however. On both occasions, US policy expressed both a conventional security interest and a broader interest in which America's security and well-being were equated generally with an international environment receptive to the nation's institutions and interests. This receptive world evidently presupposed a world in which America would be the preponderant power, able to impose, if necessary, its vision of order and stability on those who might seek to challenge that vision. The Truman Doctrine forms the most striking expression of this underlying ambiguity. By interpreting security as a function not only of a balance of power between states but of the internal order maintained by states, and not only by some states but by all states, the Truman Doctrine equated America's security with interests that clearly went well beyond conventional security requirements. Although often dismissed as mere rhetoric, this equation accurately expressed the magnitude of the nation's conception of its global role and interests from the very inception of the cold war. It also expressed the insistence with which we have identified our role and interests, however expansive, with security.

The point remains that it was a narrower and more traditional conception of security that led to the transformation of American policy from the late 1930s to the late 1940s. It was the fear that the world balance of power might shift decisively against the United States, thereby posing a direct threat to our security, that above all prompted the historic departure from isolationism to intervention. A broader definition of national interest clearly facilitated that departure. Even so, that broader interest did not form the principal, let alone the sole, mainspring of change. To put the matter differently, although the Truman Doctrine was equated from the start with the nation's security, it was a narrower conception of security that provided the principal motive for early containment policy, not only in Europe but, during the period of the Korean War, in Asia as well.

Only by assuming that the structure of American security remains essentially unchanged from what it was twenty-five years ago can one find a threat to the nation's physical security in a return to isolationism. Whereas only a generation ago it was reasonable to see America's security largely in terms of conventional balance-of-power calculations, today that view is no longer reasonable. Whereas a generation ago it was plausible to find in alliances an indispensable hedge against an uncertain future, today the indispensability of alliances is no longer plausible.

In a conventional balance-of-power system, alliances were indispensable to security for the reason that a surfeit of deterrent power was practically unachievable. In theory, it was possible for one state to acquire a degree of power sufficient to deter attack by any other state or combination of states. In practice, this ideal condition of security was seldom, if ever, attained. Nuclear-missile weapons have changed this once all-important fact of state relations. For the state that can now destroy any other state or combination of states, these weapons have in truth conferred what has heretofore proven unachievable—a surfeit of deterrent power.

It is indeed the case that in the extreme situation the great nuclear power is absolutely vulnerable with respect to its great adversary. But this ultimate vulnerability cannot be significantly reduced—let alone removed—by any alliance the great nuclear power may form. In other than the extreme situation, nuclear weapons confer a degree of security on their principal possessors that great powers seldom, if ever, enjoyed in the past. Moreover, the economic burden these weapons impose cannot be seriously compared with the strain on resources that attended the mobilization of an earlier period. The great nuclear power may live, as Raymond Aron has pointed out, "in the shadow of the apocalypse," but the shadow permits, as Aron has also noted, "bourgeois comfort and millions of automobiles." * It can no longer be seriously argued that the effort required of an isolated America to deter attack would impose a considerable—let alone an intolerable—burden on the nation's resources.

Provided that America maintains the strategic forces necessary to deter attack, alliances cannot enhance a physical security that is no longer dependent on what transpires outside the North American continent. If anything, the reverse is now the case. Although the loss of allies, even the most important allies, would not significantly alter the prospects of an adversary surviving an attack upon the United States, the risks that might have to be run on behalf of allies could lead to a nuclear con-

---

* Raymond Aron, *Peace and War: A Theory of International Relations* (New York: Doubleday, 1966), p. 304.

frontation that would escape the control of the great protagonists.

It will not do, then, to argue that if an attack by a major communist power against states to which we are most closely allied would raise the prospects of the one contingency that could threaten the nation's physical security, the defense of these allies is therefore vital to America's security. Even if America would be willing to risk nuclear war to prevent her most important allies from falling under the domination of a hostile power, the reason for taking this risk would not be security in its narrower sense. For the loss of these allies would not as such threaten America's physical security. A Soviet Union wholly in control of Western Europe would still not be a Soviet Union posing a markedly greater threat to America's physical security than the Soviet Union of today. However undesirable the other consequences of so extreme, and improbable, a situation, its consequences for security would not be comparable today with what they would have been a generation ago when security was calculated primarily in terms of geographic position, manpower, industrial concentration, etc.—that is, in terms of conventional balance-of-power calculations.

Thus, the circumstances that might still involve this nation in a nuclear war are no longer synonymous with the circumstances that might threaten its physical security. There is nothing novel in this apparent paradox of nations risking their physical existence over interests that would not jeopardize their physical existence if lost. The novelty is only the clarity with which nuclear weapons illuminate an apparent willingness to take such risks.

It is a striking illustration of the extent to which the past rules over the present that, despite the change that has occurred in the structure of American security, knowledgeable men persist in viewing this security largely in terms of a conventional balance of power. A former under secretary of state, George Ball, distinguished for his consistent opposition to the intervention in Vietnam, insists that nothing has happened in the past twenty years to change the security interest we have in the defense of Western Europe. If attacked, America must defend Western Europe with nuclear weapons, if necessary, "since encroachment on that vital industrial area would so drastically tip the power balance as to endanger our own security." *

So, too, the author of America's postwar containment policy, George Kennan, though subsequently disillusioned by the manner in which containment was implemented, has never doubted that America retains a vital security interest in preventing the industrial strength of Western Europe and Japan from falling under the control of those who would ally themselves with either the Soviet Union or China. When added to the strength of a major adversary, the military-industrial strength of Western Europe and Japan would turn the balance of world power against us. To prevent this possibility from ever materializing, Kennan has said, "is something that has lain at the heart of my thinking . . . ever since 1947." **

A leading academic critic of America's postwar globalism and of US involvement in Vietnam, Hans J. Morgenthau, insists that America's security, physical and otherwise, continues to depend today, as is has depended in the past, upon the maintenance of a balance of power both in Europe and in Asia. Morgenthau claims that in

---

* George Ball, "We Should De-escalate the Importance of Vietnam," *New York Times Magazine*, December 21, 1969, p. 31.
** Hearings before the Senate Committee on Foreign Relations, 89th Congress, 2nd Session, February 1966, p. 424.

both Europe and Asia "the United States has consistently opposed the power that threatened to make itself master of the Continent and thus gain a position that would endanger the security of the United States from across the ocean."* Although circumstances have altered, they have not invalidated this historic interest.

Even Walter Lippmann, the great iconoclast of American policy in the period of Vietnam, continues to define America's vital security interests largely in conventional terms. Although he has substantially altered the view he once entertained of the structure of the American position, Lippmann continues to find Western Europe and the area of the Caribbean vital to the nation's security. With the seizure of Cuba, he recently declared, "the vital American national interest would be involved at once."**

None of these views is convincing, let alone self-evident, if security is identified with physical security, or anything remotely approaching physical security. How would a Soviet Union in control of Europe threaten America's physical security in a way that this security cannot already be threatened today? Surely the answer is not that a Soviet Union in control of Europe would thereby possess the resources it does not possess today. Clearly it would possess additional resources, but that fact does not in any way establish a case for concluding that a thereby strengthened Soviet Union would be in a position to attack America without facing disastrous consequences. The additional strength gained through the control of Western Europe

---

* Hans J. Morgenthau, *A New Foreign Policy for the United States* (New York: Praeger Publishers, 1969), p. 193.

** Interview with Ronald Steel, *The Washington Post*, October 10, 1971, p. C–5.

would not alter the destruction the Soviet Union must in any event anticipate.

The obsolescence of the above views is all the more apparent when applied to justify American hegemony in this hemisphere. The vital interest that, in Lippmann's terms, "would be involved at once" in the event of a "seizure of Cuba" is clearly not an interest that is any longer identical with America's physical security. How would a Cuba under hostile great-power control threaten that security? We may put aside the patently absurd scenario of a great power employing Cuba as a "forward base" from which to stage a conventional attack. But is the possibility of a Cuba being used as a missile base any less absurd, in the sense that it would pose a threat to American security that did not otherwise exist? By placing missiles in Cuba, the Soviet Union would not thereby pose a greater strategic threat to America than the threat already held out by Soviet polaris-type submarines. If it is argued that by placing missiles in Cuba, the warning time of attack would be reduced from 30 minutes to 3, the answer is that Soviet submarines have already shortened this period to 3 minutes.

Were a new Cuban missile crisis to arise, its implications would in all probability be extremely grave. They would not be so, however, for the threat held out to America's physical security, but because of their enormous political and psychological impact. Even in the Soviet-American confrontation of 1962, it is far from clear that the challenge the Soviet Union posed was a challenge to America's core security. Had the Russians succeeded in keeping their missiles in Cuba, they might have been tempted to use their success to force the West out of Berlin and to break America's hegemonial position in the Western Hemisphere.

But they would not and could not have upset the nuclear balance of deterrence in such a manner as to threaten America's physical security. Today, a similar move would scarcely have even a peripheral significance for America's physical security.

American sensitivity over encroachments in her original sphere of influence may continue undiminished (witness the reaction in the fall of 1970 to Soviet moves to establish a base in Cuba for nuclear submarines), but that sensitivity must be seen in terms other than those which for a time made it imperative to exclude the military power of other great states from the hemisphere. And what may be said for the region of the Caribbean may be said with still greater force for Latin America generally.

If retention of the postwar system of commitments can be justified in terms of a narrow concept of security, the grounds for doing so must be other than conventional balance-of-power calculations. Can these grounds be found in the nuclear proliferation that would presumably attend a general American withdrawal?

The argument that such withdrawal would markedly increase the prospects of the one contingency that could threaten America's survival as a nation—a nuclear war— has been a persistent one. Indeed, it is perhaps the most pervasive and persuasive expression of the view that the world remains a very dangerous place, if anything more dangerous than ever, and that it is only the American presence, as manifested primarily by our global system of commitments, that holds these incipient dangers within tolerable proportions. Take away this presence, the argument runs, and the world will become progressively less stable, if only because, with more nations believing they must possess nuclear weapons, the prospects must increase that some among them will attempt to use these weapons to change the *status quo*. The danger of nuclear war will thereby increase as a result of nuclear proliferation, and with the increase of that danger will go the increase of the danger that America, along with the other major nuclear powers, will ultimately become involved.

The necessity for preventing nuclear proliferation therefore rests on three assumptions: that an American withdrawal would stimulate proliferation, that proliferation would increase the prospects of nuclear conflict, and that the increased prospects of nuclear conflict must increase the threat to our physical security. Of the three assumptions, the first is clearly the most plausible and, at the same time, the least important. It is not the prospects of proliferation as such but the consequences of proliferation that are crucial to the argument that the American system of commitments must not be abandoned.

Would the prime candidates for nuclear weapons prove less prudent in managing their newly acquired strength than the present nuclear powers? Would a Japan that could be destroyed by six or seven thermonuclear weapons be less prudent in managing these weapons than the Soviet Union or China? For that matter, would an Israel that could be destroyed by one or two such weapons be less prudent in its management? We have no persuasive reason for so assuming, just as we have no persuasive reason for assuming that the compulsion—or temptation—to use nuclear weapons will be greater for future nuclear powers than for present possessors of these weapons. Moreover, where a compulsion to use nuclear weapons truly exists, a compulsion to obtain them will also exist. Even if America's structure of commitments remains unchanged, can this latter compulsion be prevented in a period when nuclear power and weapons technology are becoming increasingly accessible?

Let us suppose, however, that the prospects of nuclear war are roughly proportionate to the number of states possessing nuclear weapons. Does it follow that with proliferation the danger has thereby increased of America becoming involved in a nuclear conflict? The answer depends upon the assumptions that are made about the character of American interests and, more generally, the nature of a nuclear peace. If it is assumed that America retains unchanged her present interests, then proliferation is indeed likely to increase the danger of America becoming involved in nuclear conflict. But this assumption establishes a vital American security interest in non-proliferation only by begging the question of how our vital security interests can and should be defined. If the assumption that America retains her present interests is not made, the threat to American security arising from the further spread of nuclear weapons must depend very largely upon the argument that nuclear peace is indivisible.

The argument for an indivisible nuclear peace obviously cannot be based upon historical evidence. And the fervor with which it has been put forth does not alter its necessarily speculative character. A nuclear peace may prove at least as divisible as any other peace men have known. Given the expected consequences of employing nuclear weapons, it may in fact prove even more divisible. Nor is it only the hazards of entering a nuclear war that may henceforth be expected to militate in favor of a divisible peace. Yesterday, peace was indivisible to the degree that an imbalance of military power was the possible (even the probable) price of choosing isolation from a conflict involving the other major states. Today, peace is divisible to the degree that a balance of deterrent power would be at worst unaffected, and at best improved, by choosing isolation from a nuclear conflict involving other major nuclear powers.

In a system governed by a conventional balance of power, the fear of being isolated was, with rare exception, synonymous with the fear of vulnerability to attack by superior forces. Thus, the conclusion was drawn, and hardened into dogma, that peace is indivisible, that the principal military powers must be all at peace or all at war. In a system governed by a balance of deterrent nuclear power, however, the fears of isolation and vulnerability to attack are no longer synonymous. To this extent, we must reverse what has come to be one of the received truths of the age, namely, that nuclear weapons have created a "community of fate" that precludes isolationism. Instead, the effects of these weapons have been to make peace more divisible today than it has been in a very long time.

ECONOMIC NECESSITIES

If we turn from strategic to economic realities, the case against isolationism seems no more compelling, and this despite categoric assertions that isolationism is impossible today if only because of our economic involvement abroad. Why must our economic involvement abroad preclude an isolationist policy? Surely the answer cannot simply be that this involvement has now resulted in an American dependence on the world, a dependence that may be disregarded only at the price of national well-being. For even if this presumed dependence were accepted as fact, it does not follow that a new isolationism would result in the sacrifice of our foreign economic interests. At least it does not follow unless it is assumed that the preservation of these interests is in turn dependent upon preserving the present structure of America's political-military commitments in the world.

The argument that the prosperity and, indeed, the very integrity of the American system as it is presently constituted are dependent upon preserving a hegemonial position in the world is an essential part of the radical critique of American foreign policy. In the radical view, the abandonment of this position is impossible, in the absence of fundamental change at home, because the security of an inherently expansionist economic and social system will not permit it. It is the dependence of a socio-economic order at home on the maintenance of our economic interests abroad that accounts for a policy of counterrevolutionary intervention in the Third World, just as it is the same dependence that accounts for the persistence with which America has sought to retain a predominant position in relation to the developed capitalist states. The system of formal and informal alliances is an indispensable means (though not the only means) by which American hegemony is maintained.

In the radical view, America's alliance system is an indispensable instrument for controlling others, largely to the end of America's economic advantage. In the orthodox view, this system is essential for maintaining the order and stability without which a highly interdependent world economy would be threatened. That the orthodox view positively assesses the order based on American power and refuses to acknowledge that in its economic dimensions, or elsewhere, it has operated chiefly to America's advantage is less important here than the assumption shared with the radical view that the economic interests this order presumably safeguards are indispensable to the nation's material well-being. In either view, America's dependence on her economic involvement abroad is deemed incompatible with a new isolationism.

Does the evidence bear out the argument of America's dependence on her foreign economic interests in the sense that without these interests the American economy could not function as presently constituted? It would not seem so. The US economy is remarkably self-sufficient, so much so that a policy of autarky—however undesirable its consequences to America and others—would seem to constitute an economically viable alternative. No doubt, a policy of autarky, or something closely akin to autarky, would require a period of time for the changes autarky implies to be absorbed. There are no persuasive reasons for assuming, however, that these changes could not be absorbed. Nor are there persuasive—or even plausible—reasons for assuming that these changes might have to be undertaken without the benefit of time. Only in the event of a global conflict is it reasonable to imagine the sudden and complete loss of our foreign economic interests. And, in such an event, which by definition would involve the great nuclear powers, the prospective sacrifice of foreign economic interests is likely to be the least of the catastrophes besetting the nation.

It is the sheer magnitude of the American economic involvement in the world that gives the argument of dependency a certain plausibility. Yet it is not enough simply to point to the size of foreign investment or to the volume of American exports. What is relevant in this context is the significance of these activities in relation to the domestic economy.

In 1968, gross private domestic investment was $127.7 billion, on a base of $1.6 trillion in total corporate assets.

Direct investment abroad as a percentage of total corporate investment was roughly 6 percent. In the same year, the return on total private investment abroad was $8.6 billion. When compared with domestic corporate profits of $92.3 billion, the return on foreign investment was 9.3 percent of domestic corporate profits. Exports of goods in 1968 was valued at $34.7 billion. With a gross national product (GNP) of $860 billion, the value of exports in relation to GNP was 4 percent (and in relation to the value of goods sold domestically, 8 percent). Viewed in absolute terms, the magnitude of American foreign investment and exports is quite misleading as an indication of their significance to the domestic economy.

American economic involvement abroad must be considered in terms of geographical location as well as in terms relative to the domestic economy. It is in the developed and capitalist states that the bulk of American investment is to be found, just as it is with the same states that our trade is concentrated. In 1969, these states accounted for almost 70 percent of American direct investment. In the same year they accounted for $4.2 billion of the $5.8 billion growth in the book value of direct foreign investment, contrasting with a rise of $1.2 billion in the developing areas. These figures continue a trend observable through the 1960s of a steady decline in the percentage of direct investment in poor states. Whereas in 1960 the latter had 40 percent of American direct investment, in 1969 the percentage had shrunk to 30 percent. That exports show a strikingly similar trend is only to be expected, given the character of American exports. It is our rich competitors and not the Third World nations that continue to take an ever increasing percentage of American exports while sharing an ever increasing percentage of American imports.

To this extent, therefore, there is less need to worry about the economic consequences of increased instability in the undeveloped countries, which would presumably attend a general American military withdrawal.

Consideration of the magnitude and geographical distribution of America's foreign investment and trade do not take into account America's high import rate of raw materials. How dependent is America on foreign sources of raw materials, and particularly those sources located in the Third World? Given import patterns, it has often been concluded that America is dependent upon raw material imports from the developing countries. But there is a world of difference between a dependence indicating only that imports form a high percentage of consumption and a dependence indicating the absence of any alternatives to present import patterns. The former proves no more than a relative dependence, that is, a convenience, whereas the latter proves a dependence in the strict sense of the term.

That there are alternatives to present import patterns can scarcely be disputed. What can be disputed is the degree of inconvenience they would impose, largely in terms of higher prices. In the case of most raw materials, the problem is clearly one of inconvenience, for the United States possesses most of its needed raw materials in significant quantities. Scarcity of these materials means scarcity of high-yield deposits. If and when high-yield deposits abroad should be shut off, lower yield deposits at home could presumably be exploited. How inconvenient this might prove to be in terms of cost would depend upon a number of factors. A rapidly advancing technology would almost certainly reduce significantly this inconvenience. This is true not only of metals—where technology has come to affect every aspect of production, where methods of recovery and recycling are constantly improving, and where prospects for substitutions are almost open-ended—but of practically all minerals and mineral products. In the all-important case of energy, synthetic fuels may be expected in the years to come to play an increasingly prominent role in meeting the so-called energy crisis. Indeed, the "crisis" itself must be questioned inasmuch as, for the foreseeable future, the United States has within its boundaries resources sufficient to make it quite independent of other nations for its essential energy needs. If what is presently lacking is the technology for utilizing these resources, there is reason for assuming the lack can eventually be met.

Given a sufficient period of time, then, there is the alternative of relying on our own material resources, perhaps even of doing so without great cost. But even if it were true that this alternative would prove very costly and that for at least some needed raw materials it could not be undertaken at all, it is difficult to see what bearing that prospect has on an isolationist America. At least, this is difficult to see unless it is assumed that only a continued American presence in the Third World, and a continued prospect of military intervention there, can ensure access to present sources of raw materials. In light of recent experience, however, the costs of pursuing an interventionary policy hold out every expectation of outweighing by far any reasonable expectation of material benefits.

Why, too, should we assume that revolutionary, and otherwise hostile, regimes would deny us (or, for that matter, other developed and capitalist nations) their raw materials? These regimes may be expected to exercise direct control over their natural resources and to attempt to obtain the best possible price for them. But they will still need foreign exchange to finance their own accelerating import needs, and raw material exports will still provide a principal means for obtaining foreign exchange.

The argument that developing states will shut off an isolationist and, consequently, non-interventionist America from present sources of raw materials is as absurd as the argument that once we have clearly abandoned our aspirations—or illusions—in the Third World the Soviet Union will succeed where we have failed. There is no evidence to support this argument, with its evident implication that the constraints a highly nationalistic and pluralistic world have placed on American power will not operate as well to constrain Soviet power.

Although a case for America's dependence on her economic involvement abroad cannot be sustained, it is nonetheless clear that this involvement represents a very important interest. How might a policy of isolation affect this interest with and in those states where it is chiefly concentrated? If one puts aside for the moment the possible reaction of the Soviet Union (and possibly China) to an American withdrawal, it is not easy to see why this interest should be adversely affected. At least, it is not easy to see why this interest would suffer more as a consequence of an American military withdrawal than it is likely to suffer in any event, given the present conflicts of interests between America and the states absorbing the bulk of our exports and affording the principal outlets for US foreign investment. The view that it would be so affected evidently assumes that our export and investment position must be explained on political rather than on economic grounds. Yet there is little evidence for this assumption.

Among the developed, capitalist states, to whom is trade more important? The answer can scarcely be in doubt.

Although the American economy would suffer in the event of a drying up of trade, our principal trading partners would suffer far more. In 1968, exports comprised 4 percent of the GNP of the United States, but 10 percent of the GNP of Japan, 14 percent of the GNP of the United Kingdom, and 12 percent of the GNP of Germany.*

More important, this asymmetry is reflected in the export relationships between the United States and the latter countries. In relation to our total exports, the percentages of America's exports to Japan, the United Kingdom, and Germany were 8.6 percent, 6.3 percent, and 5 percent. In turn, the percentages of the exports of these states to the United States in relation to their total exports were 32 percent, 14 percent, and 19 percent. Nor are there grounds for believing that this disparity in the relative importance of exports between America and her principal trading partners is likely to be reversed. Instead, the prospect is that the disparity will become more pronounced for an American economy that is increasingly service oriented, since the competitive advantage formerly enjoyed by goods-producing industries may be expected to decline. In any case, the present disparity of interest in trade would appear sufficient to ensure against the fear that an American military withdrawal would somehow be followed by a closing off of our principal export markets.

The American investment position in the developed countries is subject to essentially the same considerations. As in the case of trade, this position ultimately depends upon the balance of need or advantage and, of course, upon inequalities in economic power. Even so, in the case of mature economies, the charges made with respect to the

---

* In the case of Germany, the figure includes trade outside the European Economic Community.

effects of investment in undeveloped countries—that development is impeded or skewed, that scarce capital is pumped out, that labor is exploited, etc.—are largely irrelevant. So, too, is the insistence that investment must be seen as a favor conferred by, or an advantage wrenched from, others and is inseparable from a relationship of control.

Mature industrial economies cannot be controlled by foreign capital, at least not in the sense that bears a meaningful comparison to the control that may once have been exercised over undeveloped countries. It may be true that America's dominant military role in Western Europe and the role of American foreign direct investment in the North Atlantic economy are two sides of the same coin. It does not follow, however, that the role of American direct investment in Europe has been a function of our dominant military role, a role which, if abandoned, would bring an end to foreign investment.

In Japan, America's dominant military role has been no less apparent than it has been in Western Europe. Yet the Japanese have been—at least until recently—successfully resistant to American investment. If European states have been unable to resist the influx of American capital, the principal reason has been that they were unwilling to forego the advantages conferred by the innovative technology and managerial talent that have accompanied this capital. There is no persuasive reason for believing that when these advantages are either no longer apparent or are outweighed by the disadvantages attending American investment, the European states would be deterred from placing obstacles to further US investment by the prospect that, in response, the American security commitment might be withdrawn. Equally, there is no persuasive reason for believing that the withdrawal of this commitment would, in and of itself, close the door to further investment.*

Despite these considerations, the view persists that the abandonment of the postwar alliance system would lead to the breakup of the international economy into separate and competing blocs, if for no other reason than that an isolationist America would be an increasingly protectionist America. Do our alliance relationships provide, as this view apparently assumes, an indispensable incentive to compromise on issues of trade and monetary reform?

At the very least, the evidence on this point is less than clear. What is quite clear, however, is that for a number of years the consequences of alliance relationships have exacerbated economic relations between America and her major allies in that military spending abroad in support of the alliance system has been a major factor in the chronic American balance-of-payments deficit. In 1970, the net foreign exchange loss from such spending, nearly half of which was in Western Europe, came to roughly $3.4 billion. To date, the principal beneficiaries of our military expenditures abroad have shown little disposition to cover the resulting exchange loss to the United States. The present attempt to force them to do so largely through a revaluation of their currencies only promises to lead to a still larger European trade deficit with the United States. If in this situation protectionist tendencies grow and harden

---

* Does the current American effort to open the Japanese door further to foreign investment constitute an exception to the position taken above, not so much in the sense that the possibility of weakening Japanese-American security ties gives America needed leverage on the investment issue but in the sense that without such ties Japan would be much more resistant to American demands? It is possible. At the same time, American leverage on the issue of trade alone would seem quite sufficient for the investment issue as well.

in both Western Europe and America, as well they may, it will scarcely be possible to contend that the cause is an isolationist America.

To summarize the preceding discussion: It would be foolish to deny that America's foreign economic involvement represents a very significant interest. (Indeed, the evident importance of this interest is itself the most persuasive response to the fear that an isolationist America would be a protectionist—let alone an autarkic—America.) What is clearly questionable is the assertion that this involvement has resulted in America's literal dependence on the world. But even if the nation's material well-being were dependent upon its economic interests abroad, it does not follow that an American military withdrawal would jeopardize these interests. It is not in the undeveloped and unstable areas that these interests are increasingly concentrated but in the developed and capitalist countries. The argument that our economic involvement abroad precludes an isolationist policy accordingly must show that an American withdrawal would jeopardize trade and investment in Western Europe, Canada, and Japan. Clearly it would do so if we were to assume a Soviet Union in control of Western Europe and a China in control of Japan. This contingency apart for the moment (it is dealt with in the following pages), there are no compelling grounds for believing that our economic interests in the developed states rest on our alliance commitments. These interests primarily reflect reciprocal economic advantage rather than America's military hegemony. As such, they appear no more vulnerable in a world in which the American alliance structure has been dismantled than in a world in which America maintains its present commitments.

IV THE POSSIBILITY OF A NEW ISOLATIONISM: THE BROADER DIMENSIONS OF SECURITY

SINCE NEITHER STRATEGIC NOR ECONOMIC NECESSITIES preclude the withdrawal from security commitments that America has made over the past generation, a new isolationism is possible. But would it be desirable? The effects of withdrawal need not be accepted simply because they would no longer threaten the nation's physical security and material well-being. They may for other reasons prove sufficiently undesirable to justify retaining intact the essential structure of America's postwar commitments. Although an isolationist policy no longer holds out the adverse consequences it once did, the consequences it may hold out cannot and should not be discounted.

Even in an earlier period, America abandoned isolationism not simply because a fascist victory was thought to threaten the nation's physical security. A fascist victory also threatened the nation's greater-than-physical security since it carried the prospect of a world in which America's political and economic frontiers would have to become coterminous with her territorial frontiers, a world in which societies that shared our culture, institutions, and values might very possibly disappear—in sum, a world in which the American example and American influence would become irrelevant. In such a world, men argued, America would find it difficult, if not impossible, to realize her promise, since a hostile world from which America was shut out would inevitably affect the integrity of the nation's institutions and the quality of its domestic life. The issues of physical security and economic well-being apart, it was to prevent this prospect from materializing that the nation abandoned its interwar isolationism, intervened in World War II, and, in the years following the war, adopted a policy of containment.

Would the prevention of a similar prospect make a new isolationism undesirable? The question is little more than rhetorical. Provided that the likely consequences of an American withdrawal were to approximate the consequences sketched out above, a new isolationism would evidently prove undesirable. The issue, of course, is not here but in the view that these consequences are likely or even plausible following an American withdrawal. Yet, unless one piles tenuous assumption upon tenuous assumption respecting the consequences of an American withdrawal, the implausible character of this view becomes apparent almost in its mere statement. For it requires us to ignore the most significant changes that have occurred in the world since the last great war, changes that have not only transformed the bases of America's physical security but of her security in the greater-than-physical sense as well.

In part, these changes in America's greater-than-physical security stem from the very changes that have transformed the bases of her physical security. Whereas in an earlier period it was still entirely possible to imagine an imbalance of power sufficient to result in a security problem the solution of which would seriously affect the nation's political institutions and the general quality of its domestic life, today this contingency is, at best, very remote. For the military forces in being that were once required in an age of conventional warfare to defend against attack are no longer required, just as the portion of the nation's material resources that were once required for defense of the homeland are no longer required. To this extent, at least, America could exist as an island in a hostile world with consequences to her internal polity that can scarcely be compared to the internal consequences feared in the 1930s.

In part, the changes in America's greater-than-physical security are also the consequences of constraints that have emerged to limit the use of force, particularly by the great powers.* In their mutual relations, it has long been apparent that the great nuclear powers are inhibited by the common realization of the dangers inherent in direct confrontation. In their relations with the weak, the strong are also inhibited, however, by the ever rising costs of employing force. As against a population determined to resist, the costs of military conquest and pacification have become exorbitant. They have become exorbitant not only because of the politicization of peoples but because of the growing conviction that force is no longer a legitimate instrument of national policy save when employed in self-defense or in pursuit of liberation from an alien and oppressive rule.

These constraints clearly do not justify the conclusion that force is no longer a useful, let alone a usable, instru-

---

* These constraints not only limit the use of military power but of other forms of power as well. I emphasize the constraints on military power since it is here that change has been the most marked and the most significant.

ment of national policy. They do support the view that the utility of force has sharply declined and that it has done so in a very brief period. The measure of this transformation is strikingly illustrated when we recall the expectations of military power entertained scarcely more than three decades ago. In the 1930s, the fear of a fascist victory was equated with the fear of a pattern of expansion that, once completed in Europe, would extend to Latin America. It is important not to see this fear of yesterday in the light of contemporary expectations. The world of the late 1930s was still very much a traditional world in which expansion was equated largely with territorial conquest, or the functional equivalent thereof, and not with the precarious forms of influence that we have since become accustomed to (and all too frequently mistakenly equate with control). Certainly, direct territorial expansion was the preferred mode of the Axis powers. In these circumstances, a hostile world would indeed have meant a world from which America would have been literally shut out. Moreover, given the expectation that pacification following military conquest would not prove too difficult, it followed that territorial expansion conferred additional power, whether in industrial plant, natural resources, population, or strategic position.

Nor did the fears and expectations that were associated with the expansionist goals of the Axis powers materially abate in the period immediately following the war. Even where the Soviet Union showed little inclination to undertake a course of territorial conquest, it was widely assumed that expansion through indirect methods would prove quite as effective and durable as the direct control the Russians exercised in areas occupied by the Red Army. However misplaced this assumption may appear in retrospect, it did not appear so at a time when an exhausted Western Europe resembled nothing so much as a huge political and social vacuum; when western communist parties, apparently subordinated to Soviet interests, possessed considerable strength and attractiveness; when national assertiveness in Europe seemed to have disappeared, while elsewhere it had yet to appear; and when the example of the Soviet Union had—as until the early 1950s it would continue to have—considerable appeal.

In these circumstances, the expansion of communism by whatever methods was not only equated with the expansion of Soviet power but was seen to hold out the same ultimate prospect that the fascist powers had earlier held out.* Nor did this belief moderate after the initial years of the cold war. If anything, it intensified as the cold war intensified, and this despite the fact that the increasing difficulty of translating not only military power but other forms of power as well into reliable influence (let alone control) antedated the abatement of the classic cold war in the early 1960s. Yet the very factors that were ultimately to lead to an abatement of the cold war were in large measure the same factors that contributed to the growing separation

---

* To the circumstances noted above must of course be added the intensity of the ideological issue. From the outset of the cold war, anti-communism assumed a significance that on an earlier occasion anti-fascism scarcely assumed even after we were at war. In retrospect, it is easy and fashionable to point to these greater fears that communism evoked and to find in the American reaction to Stalin's Russia an almost hysterical exaggeration of the devil's strengths. It should be recalled, however, that, given the character of fascist ideology, fascism could never be seen as a serious alternative to the American example, whereas the Soviet example did appear as such an alternative. Moreover, the face of Stalinism was at once frightening and awe-inspiring—so much so that subsequent Soviet gains in material power have never quite compensated for the loss of these qualities in the post-Stalin period.

between power and influence.

There is no need to review again the changes that have transformed the world of the 1930s and 1940s and that have contributed to the growing constraints on the use of power by the great states, whether against each other or against small states. What is important to stress here is the result these changes have had in substantially modifying, if not in removing altogether, the prospect that in an earlier period gave rise to apprehensions over the nation's greater-than-physical security. The fear that could once be seriously entertained—the fear that a hostile power or combination of powers might succeed in uniting a world from which America would be effectively shut out—can no longer be seriously entertained.

THE THIRD WORLD

Thus, the similar prospect taken with the utmost seriousness only a decade ago, that a hostile power or combination of powers might succeed in shutting America off from the nations of the Third World, is no longer a serious concern. Nor is this conclusion any longer a matter of widespread dispute. Here, at any rate, what was deemed the purest of heresy yesterday has become near orthodoxy today.

If the present administration does not acknowledge an essential change in the definition of American interests in the Third World, it does accept the view that the threat to those interests has diminished. A pluralistic world, though far more complicated than the world of a generation ago, is nevertheless held to be a safer world. Interpreted, in essence, as the triumph of nationalism, pluralism not only means that communist expansion in the undeveloped nations no longer carries the threat to America it once carried; it also means that the prospect of communist expansion has dramatically declined. So, too, it is concluded that there has been a marked decline in the need for military intervention in the Third World in order to preserve a global order compatible with American interests.

The optimism reflected in this view is not without limits, however. To the extent that a policy of non-intervention has been adopted in relation to the Third World, it is still contingent upon the assumption that the consequences of such a policy will not lead to marked instability or to the substantial reduction of American influence. The fears of yesterday have surely receded, but they have by no means disappeared. Thus, the decision to withdraw from commitments made in the Third World is not taken and, indeed, is explicitly disavowed.

Yet there is no persuasive reason for believing that an American withdrawal, though it might well result in greater instability and in a diminution of influence, would also result in an America denied access to the Third World, whether because of the independent initiatives of hostile revolutionary regimes or, more importantly, because of the influence exercised by other and hostile great powers. The first projection must assume that the undeveloped states have less need—particularly less economic need—of America than America has need of them, whereas the reverse is the case. The second projection must assume that the failures attending American policy in the Third World over the past decade would not attend the policies of rival great powers, and that the resistance shown to American interventionary actions would not be shown to similar actions by others. There is little in the record that lends support to this assumption.

If the Soviet Union's record in the Third World does not

suffer by comparison with our own, it is largely for the reason that the Russians have not—or not yet—been tempted by their military capabilities to undertake the vast designs we were tempted to undertake. Naval power apart, the Soviet Union could deny us access to areas of the undeveloped world only if the influence it exercised there were reliable. Yet the one lesson we should have learned from the experience of the recent past is the unreliability of influence, let alone of control, in these areas. There is no need to impose constraints on Soviet behavior in the Third World, even if we were still in a position to do so with some promise of success, for there are constraints enough without our efforts. Indeed, the relatively few states where the Russians do enjoy a marked influence—Cuba, Egypt, North Vietnam, India—support the conclusion that Soviet success has come about because of rather than despite American policies.

Whatever the ambiguities that continue to mark both outlook and policy toward the Third World, there has been change. The extent of the change awaits a meaningful test. Even so, it is no longer in relation to the Third World but in relation to Western Europe and Japan that the desirability of an isolationist America is rejected out of hand.

JAPAN

In Asia, Japan forms the great exception to the insistence of most critics of American policy that we must disengage, however gradually, from our present commitments. Is it feasible, however, to do both, to withdraw elsewhere in Asia while retaining the basic commitment to Japan? The view that it is feasible must assume either that the Japanese would continue to shun the development of a military force to protect their overseas interests or that, while developing such a force, they would nevertheless remain content to rely on the American nuclear guarantee.

Neither assumption seems plausible. An American withdrawal elsewhere in Asia will almost surely push the Japanese in the direction of developing a conventional military capability quite different from the limited capability they possess today. Having done so, however, is it reasonable to suppose that Japan would be content to remain without the ultimate instruments—or symbols—of sovereignty in the nuclear age? And even if the Japanese were content to do so, would it be desirable to provide an American nuclear umbrella for Japan without the assurance that America could continue to determine the circumstances in which that umbrella would become meaningful? It may of course be argued either that these circumstances would not arise or that if they were to arise there would be an essential coincidence of American and Japanese interests. The latter argument suggests the quite unlikely prospect of a Japan that can be relied upon to remain subservient to American interests. The former argument suggests that, after all, the nuclear guarantee itself has little, if any, meaning.

Quite apart from the difficulties inherent in a policy that disengages elsewhere in Asia while retaining the basic commitment to Japan, there is the broader issue of the purpose served by keeping untouched the cornerstone of America's postwar Asian policy. In its origins, the purpose of the security commitment to Japan was largely coincidental with the purpose of containment as applied to Asia.

In defining the American defense perimeter in the Pacific as extending to the Ryukyus, American policy simply followed the logic of the growing conflict with the Soviet Union. The events of the late 1940s and early 1950s—above all, the Chinese communist accession to power and the Korean War—were seen as confirming and immeasurably strengthening the policy of guaranteeing the security of Japan. Without American power, the argument ran, there was nothing to counter the power of an aggressive and expansionist China allied to an equally aggressive and expansionist Soviet Union. The Sino-Soviet alliance threatened at once to overturn the Asian balance of power and, in doing so, to pose a direct danger to Japan. The Korean War provided a striking confirmation of this analysis. It resolved any remaining doubts over the need to guarantee Japanese security.

Nor were such doubts revived a decade after Korea, in the period following the Cuban missile crisis, when the intense conflict between the United States and the Soviet Union began to abate, when Japan had fully recovered from the war and was moving to her present position of economic preponderance in Asia, and when the last semblance of any pretense to unity between the major communist powers was dropped and intense rivalry openly acknowledged. Despite these changes, the purpose of the security commitment to Japan presumably remained coincidental with the purpose of containment, only it was now China that formed the prime object of containment in Asia.

The equation that can only evoke an embarrassed silence today—that the maintenance of an Asian balance of power was identical with the containment of China—provided a principal rationale for US intervention in Vietnam. Moreover, although many critics of the intervention rejected the application of the equation to Vietnam, they did not reject the equation itself. For this reason, the debate over Vietnam (and the larger debate over America's Asian policy as well) turned largely around the issue of the nature of

the Chinese threat and the appropriate means for counter-
ing this threat, but not whether the threat—particularly
if it were to take the form of direct expansion—should be
countered by American power.

It is only in very recent years that the realization has
slowly dawned that a balance of power already exists in
Asia, that it has existed for some time, that it can be increasingly maintained by Asian powers, and that China
does not have and cannot be expected in the foreseeable
future to have the power to challenge, let alone to overturn, this indigenous balance.

In these circumstances, what is the purpose served by the
American security commitment to Japan? Is it any longer
plausible to argue that this purpose is to prevent Chinese
dominance over Japan, given Japan's power, actual and
latent, and given the Soviet Union's interest in constraining
the power and influence of China? It would not seem so.
Instead, a meaningful Chinese threat to Japan's security
appears among the most implausible of prospects even (one
is tempted to say, especially) in the absence of the American commitment. Not only would it provoke intense Soviet
opposition, and this all the more so if Japan were no longer
tied to the United States, but it would also risk impelling
Japan to acquire nuclear weapons—or, since a nuclear
Japan is in any event a likelihood, it would drastically
foreshorten the period in which Japan would become a
nuclear power. Substantially the same considerations must
apply to the prospect of a threat to Japan's vital interests
emanating from the Soviet Union, but with the substitu-
tion of Chinese for Soviet opposition. Are we left, then,
with an American commitment, the real purpose of which
is no longer to provide an indispensable counterweight
either to China or to Russia but rather to preserve other

American interests in Asia by keeping a residual control over Japanese actions?

From whatever vantage point one views the present Asian power structure, the conclusion seems inescapable that the security commitment to Japan has lost its original, though still avowed, *raison d'etre*. Nor is it easy to make a persuasive case for the different, and unavowed, purpose of maintaining leverage over Japan's future behavior. At least, it is not easy to do so save for those reasons which have always made states of imperial proportions and pretensions resistant to change that challenges their preponderant role.

A Japan in possession of nuclear weapons and no longer tied to the United States would still be a Japan constrained to behave moderately in Asia. Japan's possession of nuclear weapons would confer an independence of action Japan does not presently enjoy. It would not alter the extreme vulnerability of Japan to nuclear destruction. The Chinese fear, however understandable on historical grounds, that a rearmed Japan would once again behave toward China as it did in the past, can have no reasonable basis. Toward Southeast Asia as well, the Japanese no longer have either the opportunity or the incentive to act as they once acted. On the contrary, they have every reason today to act with moderation.

If these considerations are at all convincing, the case against abandoning the system of postwar commitments is narrowed to Western Europe. A new isolationism might stop short of Europe and thus take the form of a geographical reversal of interwar isolationism. Whereas the old isolationism did not apply to Latin America and retained a measure of ambiguity toward Asia, a new isolationism might stop short of Europe while centering on Asia and extending to Latin America as well. Indeed, were America only to withdraw from her present commitments in Asia, the change would constitute something akin to a revolution in postwar policy (especially since it is Asia that has provided for more than two decades the principal bone of contention in American diplomacy). Nor does it follow that if we choose to adopt an isolationist policy toward some areas we have no choice but to do the same toward all areas. The assertion is no more persuasive than the assumption it so evidently reflects: that American commitments (and interests) form an integral whole that cannot survive the disappearance of any of its component parts.

WESTERN EUROPE

That the American interest in Europe must be set apart from American interests elsewhere is a proposition bordering on the self-evident. It is not only the industrial power of Western Europe, and the large American stake in this power, that give this region a unique significance. The nations of Western Europe hold a unique significance for America by virtue of their political and cultural affinity with this nation. Despite the mixture of sentimentalism and paternalism that has long marked American attitudes toward Asia (and, above all, toward China), and despite the curious belief that an "innocent" Asia would prove receptive to the American example (in contrast to a resistant and rather decadent Europe), at the critical junctures the supreme importance of Europe to America for reasons other than power has been apparent. An America shut out of Asia would not be an America shut out from societies that begot and that continue to nourish our culture and institutions. The same cannot be said of an America shut out of Europe. Although a hostile Europe would not increase the present threat to America's physical security, in other respects such a development would surely have a profound impact on the nation.

Just as there is no meaningful comparison between the significance of American interests in Europe and in Asia, there is no meaningful comparison between the circumstances attending an American withdrawal from Europe and an American withdrawal from Asia. Whereas in Asia an indigenous balance of power already exists—or very nearly so—in the triangular relationship of Japan, China, and Russia, in Europe an indigenous balance of power does not yet exist. Whereas in Asia the problem of completing the nuclear triangle is one that will ultimately be resolved by Japan alone, in Europe the problem of providing for an effective nuclear deterrent is one that must be resolved by several nations which still bear the burden of a long tradition of competition and rivalry. Finally, whereas in Asia America's major alliance commitment is with an insular nation that World War II left geographically intact, in Europe America is allied to states that are accessible by land to Soviet power and the largest of which remains divided as a result of defeat in war.

It is therefore not only the distinctive character of our interests in Europe that presumably forbids applying to Europe a logic of withdrawal that may appear persuasive elsewhere; it is also the distinctive character of the European setting in which this logic would have to be applied. When interest and circumstance are taken together, the all-too-familiar argument runs, the only conclusion to be drawn is one that precludes any substantial change in the American relationship to Western Europe until such time as circumstance itself safely permits such change. What form this altered circumstance must take is usually defined in terms—a united Germany within a united Western Europe—that would not only make America's dominant military role in Western Europe glaringly superfluous but indeed impossible.

The point at issue, then, is not the importance of Europe to America, but the policy that holds out the greatest promise of resulting in both a militarily independent and friendly Europe. Whatever the apparent disposition of the major Western European governments today, the wisdom of retaining America's postwar military role in Europe must be insistently challenged. For that role perpetuates a symbiotic relationship that Europe's resources and strength make unnecessary and that must eventually lead to resentment and recrimination on both sides if it is not substantially altered.

There is no need to review once again the detailed reasoning that must presumably rule out any serious alteration in, let alone the abandonment of, the American alliance relationship to Western Europe. What is impressive is that the thorough familiarity of this argument has bred neither contempt nor a demand for substantial change among most observers otherwise critical of American foreign policy.

To be sure, there is the increasingly widespread (though still far from prevalent) view that we must reduce the size of our conventional forces in Europe. But the demand to reduce American forces is seldom accompanied by any expressed conviction that such reduction should be seen as only a first step toward forging a basic change in our relationship with Western Europe. Instead, the purpose of reducing American forces—whether by a quarter, a third, or even a half—is generally held to be entirely compatible with our current relationship, the principal merits of the cutback being that it would improve the American balance-of-payments position while providing the Europeans with an incentive to assume a still greater share of the burden of their own defense. (Of course, another merit is obviously implicit in the nature of the proposal itself—that it would cut down on the size of our military presence abroad.)

Within this accepted framework, the balance of advantage in the argument over troop reduction in Europe remains unclear. It does so not because we would thereby be giving up an important bargaining chip with the Soviet Union, but because a reduction is likely to stimulate further doubt among Europeans about the credibility of the American nuclear guarantee while failing to provide the incentive to obtain a greater independence from America. It is likely to stimulate further doubt about the American guarantee for the same reason that doubt already exists. It is likely to fail to provide the incentive to greater independence for the same reason that this incentive is largely absent today. A troop reduction would reinforce the skepticism that in the extreme situation America will be willing to sacrifice itself for Europe. At the same time, it would leave unaltered the sense of impotence that results from a continued dependence upon America for the ultimate means of protection.

Would the incentive for the Western European nations to provide for their own security result from what is only rarely urged—a total withdrawal of American forces from Europe? Withdrawal of all American forces would carry with it withdrawal of the tactical nuclear weapons under American control. If both conventional forces and nuclear weapons were removed, the credibility of the American guarantee would very probably be reduced to a hollow shell. In these circumstances, would the major European states do for themselves and for each other what they have continued to expect—even while doubting—that America would do for them collectively? If the answer were clearly yes, then the way would be just as clearly opened to a European nuclear force that would remove the reason for the alliance. It must be admitted, however, that the answer remains unclear, despite the anomaly of a France (or Great Britain) that may be unwilling to risk its existence for Germany while reckoning on an America that is supposedly willing to do so.

If a partial withdrawal of American conventional forces would not essentially change the problems attending the European alliance, and might even worsen them, while a total withdrawal would force an unpredictable moment of truth, does a middle ground exist? Is it feasible to conceive of a relationship that would at once give the Western European states ultimate control over their destinies while preserving the American guarantee? Only, it would seem, in the limited sense of an interim solution facilitating the transition from the old dispensation to the new. The Western Europeans cannot provide for their own security without adequate nuclear forces. With such forces, however, why should they continue to need the American guarantee?

It scarcely seems sufficient to reply that the alliance with America would still serve as an indispensable backstop to the defense systems of the Western European nations. An indispensable backstop against what? Is it necessary to be able to threaten the destruction of the principal Soviet cities several times over to insure that the Russians will refrain from aggressive behavior against Western Europe? The backstop notion is either a euphemism to conceal the circumstances in which the American guarantee would come to an end, or it is meaningless. And even if it were granted that an independent Western Europe might still desire an American backstop, would we be willing to provide one when we no longer controlled Europe's defenses and Europe's actions? If it is hard enough today to see America risking its cities for Europe, is it not rather fanciful to see our doing so in these changed circumstances?

The point seems clear enough: either our dominant military position in relation to Western Europe remains, or the alliance eventually lapses, in effect if not in form. There is not and cannot be anything that even approximates a partnership of equals between Europe and America without an adequate European nuclear force. But with such a force there will be neither the need nor, in all probability, the desire for partnership in security.

The proposal that America end its military hegemony in Europe must therefore be seen without illusions. Moreover, the possible consequences of an American withdrawal from Europe and the lapse, sooner or later, of the American guarantee ought not to be sugarcoated either by emphasizing only the baneful effects of American dominance or by assuming a Soviet response to an American withdrawal we have no right to assume.

It is not enough to say that American dominance has been an obstacle in the path to greater European unity, without acknowledging at the same time that the removal of this obstacle may lead to the breakdown of that degree of unity Europe presently enjoys. Nor will it do to argue that it has been the American military presence in Europe that has kept the Russians in Central Europe and thereby prolonged the division of Germany and the continent. We have no persuasive reasons for assuming (though it would make matters far easier if we had) that the Russians would give up their position in Europe and agree to a satisfactory solution of Germany's division in return for an American withdrawal. On the contrary, we must assume that the Russians will stay where they are whether the Americans stay or go.

However one views the origins and early years of the cold war, the point remains that the Russian position in Europe today is not simply a function of, or a response to, the American position. In some part, of course, it is just that. In large part, however, the Soviet position is identified with interests that are inseparable not only from imperial security—that is, the security of the Soviet sphere of control in Eastern and Central Europe—but from the structure of power within the Soviet Union itself.

As the Soviet response to the events in Czechoslovakia in 1968 strongly suggests, the degree of change in Europe that the Russians can be expected to accept is limited by what they believe would threaten their domestic security. Czechoslovakia was surely seen to raise a threat to imperial security. But above and beyond this threat loomed the even more terrifying prospect that the twin viruses of liberalization and national independence might spread to the Soviet Union, thereby threatening the structure of Soviet power and the very integrity of the Soviet state. If a similar prospect would attend a Soviet withdrawal from Central Europe, as presumably it would, it is difficult to see what might induce the present Soviet leadership, or, for that matter, any foreseeable Soviet leadership, to abandon its present position.*

---

* It is not necessary to account for the Czech intervention primarily in terms of the character of the present Soviet leadership and its particular preoccupations. The circumstances preceding and attending the intervention would have provoked, in all likelihood, a similar response by any Soviet leadership, at least any that we have experi-

In the end, the case for an American withdrawal from Europe rests primarily upon what the major Western European states are willing to do for themselves and, of course, for each other. The view that they would be willing to do very little, even in the face of an American withdrawal, ignores what they have already done in maintaining substantial conventional forces. It also ignores the extent to which American policies, while ostensibly encouraging the Western Europeans to make a greater effort on their own behalf, have eroded the will to do so by virtue of our own military hegemony.

It is always possible that an American withdrawal would find each of the major European states running to make its own separate accommodation with the Russians. Given the resources the Western Europeans possess to defend themselves, however, is this a plausible outcome, particularly if an American withdrawal is staged quite gradually and is attended by substantial American efforts to aid in the establishment of a credible European nuclear force? * The

---

enced. The interests in the defense of which the intervention was undertaken, interests which in the end could scarcely be preserved save by intervention, are not the unique possession of the present leadership. Moreover, given the importance of these interests, the intervention does not invalidate the general points we have made concerning the growing constraints on the use of force against small powers. What it confirms, if confirmation were needed, is that there remain interests for which the great powers will still use force. In retrospect, what is impressive is that, in view of the critical interests that were at stake, Soviet leadership proved so hesitant and vacillating about intervening.

* There is a considerable difference between simple withdrawal of American forces and a withdrawal that is attended by American efforts to provide for Europe's military independence. To be sure, in either case a risk is run. Even so, in the latter case, a strong incentive is provided recipient states to make the necessary effort to achieve military independence, particularly when the prospect of assistance is accompanied by the prospect of the American guarantee lapsing after a transitional period.

basis for such a force already exists in the respective British and French nuclear forces. It is quite true that, even making the most optimistic assumptions, a coordinated British-French nuclear force could not begin to rival that of the Russians. But there is no reason why it need do so unless one posits a Soviet Union yearning to attack Western Europe and prevented from doing so only by the prospect of utter destruction. If one accepts this view, then any realistic projection of a European nuclear force must prove inadequate for deterrence. But so must the long-term credibility of the American guarantee now that the Soviet Union enjoys strategic parity with the United States.

It is another matter to argue that, despite a credible though modest European nuclear force, the Russians would still have the incentive to behave immoderately in the event that West Germany sought to acquire her own nuclear arms. Even this one contingency, though it must be taken seriously, may be exaggerated. Despite continuing prophesies of a preventive strike against Chinese nuclear and missile installations, the Russians have permitted the development of a strategic force by their great neighbor to the east whom they have at least as much reason to fear as a nuclear-armed West Germany.

The point remains that Germany in possession of, or seeking to possess, nuclear weapons would arouse the strongest opposition not only of the Soviet Union but of Germany's allies as well. Provided the Germans obtain a reasonable security from a European nuclear force, why should they wish to undertake a course of action that would isolate them from their allies in the West—states with which Germany's prosperity is firmly tied—while dashing whatever modest prospects are held out by an evolving *Ostpolitik?*

There is one consequence, however, that an American withdrawal from Europe is likely to evoke. An American withdrawal, even in favorable circumstances, would result in a decrease of American influence and in an increase of Russian influence over European affairs. This consequence must be expected even if we assume, as it seems only reasonable to assume, that Russia will be increasingly preoccupied with her great rival to the east. The fears of a generation ago of a hostile world from which the United States would be shut out are of diminishing relevance, if indeed they retain any relevance at all. It is not, then, the issue of America's greater-than-physical security (let alone the issue of her physical security) that is directly raised by an American withdrawal from Europe, but the issue of America's paramount influence in Europe. It is the same issue that is raised by an American withdrawal elsewhere in the world.

V THE PRICE OF ISOLATIONISM

THE ANALYSIS DRAWN IN THE PRECEDING PAGES has relied
to a considerable degree upon a view of the world in which
the great powers are increasingly constrained in their behavior, whether toward each other or toward small powers.
These constraints are not the result of any shared vision
of the world. They are not, for the most part, sustained
through trust. Even so, to the extent that they prove effective, they are constitutive of order, however rudimentary
and, in many ways, unsatisfactory this order may be.

Within this order, I have argued, an isolationist America
is possible. It is possible, moreover, without evoking the
prospect of a Fortress America. An isolationist America
would not be an isolated America. It would not be an
America alone in a hostile world. Nor would it be an
America that has ceased to play a significant role in the
world. Whatever the merits of the familiar theme that
great power must give rise to great responsibility, it is certainly the case that by virtue of her power America would
of necessity continue to play a significant role in the world.
Indeed, the mere presence of this power must in itself
continue to be a source of restraint for others, since a new
isolationism would afford no guarantee to others that re-

gardless of how they behaved American power could be discounted.*

The argument therefore assumes—it seems hardly necessary to make the point—that American strategic power would remain. It further assumes that American naval power, strategic and conventional, would remain. Naval power would no longer be employed, as it has been employed in the past, in support of land operations, whether by American forces or by the forces of indigenous powers. (The advantage heretofore conferred by America's unquestioned superiority at sea—to intervene at times and places of our own choosing—is in any event brought increasingly into question by the rapid growth of Soviet naval power.) Naval power would be employed to ensure the free use of the seas. The withdrawal from commitments on land in no way reduces the need to retain sufficient naval power to move unhindered at sea. However improbable the contingency of denial of free movement of US ships at sea, that contingency must be guarded against.

The risks a new isolationism entails, then, are not risks to America's core security. Nor is there a substantial risk to America's greater-than-physical security. This is not to say that there are no risks or no costs to a new isolationism.

---

* It is often argued that the principal danger of withdrawing, whether in Europe or in Asia, is that once we have gotten out it will prove difficult, if not impossible, ever to go back should circumstances require our going back. This argument is not without significance for the light it throws on the nature and purpose of the American alliance system today. Why should it prove so difficult to go back if the security of former allies is seriously threatened? Surely the reason would not be the diffidence of former allies. Nor, presumably, would the reason be the diffidence of America confronted by the prospect of a hostile world. In these circumstances, there is no reason to assume a lack of incentive on the part of either side to re-establish a lapsed relationship.

Although the world of an isolationist America would still be a world with order, it would clearly not be the order we have dreamed of and sought to establish, particularly since World War II. It would not be an order over which American power presided. Nor would it be an order holding out the promise of a world moving progressively, under American leadership, toward the ultimate triumph of liberal-capitalist values. The price of a new isolationism is that America would have to abandon its aspirations to an order that has become synonymous with the nation's vision of its role in history. The price of isolationism today is to be found above all in the prospect of a world in which American influence, though still considerable, would markedly decline.

It is this prospect of a reduced American role that successive administrations have insistently identified as a threat to the nation's security, just as it is the same prospect that has prompted the pursuit of an interventionist policy. The critics of US foreign policy, both radical and conventional, have obscured this point. Radical criticism has been unable consistently to accept the view that America's fear of losing a preponderant position may be due to reasons other than the fear of no longer enjoying the material benefits preponderance confers. Yet conventional criticism also misses the mark in attributing an interventionist policy to false perceptions or to a ritualistic anti-communism. An emphasis on an inability among policy-makers to recognize and to accept the world for what it is gives to American policy a quality of disinterestedness it does not possess and a quality of innocence it does not have.

Emphasis on ritualistic anti-communism, though surely important in any account of the support public opinion has afforded American policy, obscures the significance of

other, and possibly stronger, motives impelling those re-
sponsible for policy. America's anti-communism is to be
explained as much in terms of the will to retain influence
over others as it is to be explained in terms of an ideological obsession that is supposedly divorced from interest and
blind to political realities. Opposition to radical revolution
in the Third World is to be explained as much by the expectation that such revolution, if successful, will prove
resistant to American influence as by the fact that the
revolution is radical.

In very different circumstances, and with equally different consequences, it is this same reluctance to relinquish
established positions of preponderance that accounts for
American opposition to change in alliance relationships
with the economically developed nations. It is this continued reluctance today that largely accounts for the devotion to "partnerships" without equality, "regionalism"
without dominant regional powers, and change without
instability. (In part, of course, the fear of instability must be
traced to the conviction that peace is indivisible. Instability is identified with increased prospects of war. It is not
change, then, but peaceful and stable change that we presumably support. Not surprisingly, many view our devotion to peaceful and stable change as, in effect, a commitment to maintaining the *status quo*.)

The question persists whether the nation can abandon
the role it has played since World War II without corrosive
effects for its domestic life. For the abandonment of that
role will result in a greater influence of others. In Europe
and Japan, the abandonment of the American alliance
system and the withdrawal of American forces, though
gradually staged, must be expected to enhance the influence of the Soviet Union and China. In the Third World,

a similar prospect must be entertained despite the fact that here the competition for influence has become an increasingly expensive game that is increasingly devoid of durable consequences. The point remains that great powers continue to attach significance to this game, however evanescent its stakes may have become.

Nor is it plausible to expect that the loss in influence resulting from an American withdrawal would be compensated by the gain in influence resulting from the example we might set at home. At the height of the controversy over Vietnam, it was fashionable for critics of the war to urge that we could accomplish by the force of our example at home what we could not accomplish by the force of our arms abroad. It is not surprising that with the passage of time this argument seems to have lost much of its appeal. It is by now apparent that even if men were more influenced by example than by precept, our example is not very relevant to the developing states. Nor is it true that in the relations of nations example is a more effective means of influence than precept. Although it may be persuasively argued that precept itself has become increasingly ineffective as a means of influence in a very pluralistic world, it is another matter to contend that example represents an adequate substitute.

Would the realization that the nation had settled for a far more modest role in the world prove internally debilitating? In the wake of a war that has had deeply corrosive domestic effects, the question must seem absurd. It is by no means so. There is nothing self-evident about the conviction, so central to isolationist thought in the past, that places an almost consistently negative assessment on the domestic effects of foreign policy, and particularly one holding out the constant prospect of military intervention.

To the extent that this conviction has been revived to-day, it has been applied not only to the period of Vietnam but to the long generation of cold war as well. Yet the view that finds the domestic effects of the cold war debilitating necessarily rests upon a comparison of what has happened with what might have happened, upon a comparison of what was done to improve the quality of domestic life with what might have been done if a preoccupation with the state's security and preponderant role in the world had not been paramount. That juxtaposition proves very little, however, since we can have no assurance that what might have been done in the absence of the pressures engendered by the cold war would in fact have been done. All we can say with assurance about this period is that much of the impetus for domestic change, the desirability of which is generally acknowledged today, was in part provided by the hegemonial competition that marked the cold war. No doubt, this conclusion—with its suggestion that, on balance, the domestic effects of the cold war may have been salutary—will strike many as perverse. Whether perverse or not, it appears at least as plausible as the contrary conclusion.

There is no reliable generalization that can be made independent of time and circumstance about the relationship between foreign and domestic policy. But if the experience of the cold war suggests that this relationship is not always negative, the experience of Vietnam affords a striking illustration of the circumstances in which it will be so. Although the domestic effects of the war are often exaggerated out of all proportion, the undisputed point remains that Vietnam has had debilitating effects at home. Even if it is assumed that the future costs of maintaining America's present role and interests in the world will not prove as exorbitant as the war in Vietnam, these costs will still prove considerable. For the world is more recalcitrant today than ever. It is also more unmanageable than ever because the restraints on the use of power by the would-be guardians of order are greater than they have ever been.

VI PROSPECTS
FOR A NEW ISOLATIONISM

WILL THE DOMESTIC EFFECTS of the Vietnam War lead to a
new isolationism? And if not to a new isolationism, then
at least to a far more modest world role for the United
States?

The answers to these questions remain almost as uncertain today as they did at the outset of the Nixon administration. After three years of speculation, it is still unclear
whether, in retrospect, Vietnam will be seen as the transitional event leading to a more mature and discriminate,
though substantially unchanged, foreign policy or as the
initial, though decisive, turn to a very different policy.
Although Vietnam appears as a momentous event in
American foreign policy, and, indeed, in America's history,
at this juncture there is still no apparent way of definitively
assessing the war's lasting internal effects.

This uncertainty holds even for the group whose views
have been most sharply affected by the experience of Viet-

nam—the elite young.* There is no way of knowing what
the long-term consequences of the war will be on the leadership of the younger generation. It is always possible that
time alone will moderate the prevailing outlook—an outlook that, whatever the term used to describe it, suggests a
new isolationism by virtue of its pervasive rejection of
further military involvement abroad, its confidence that
American security does not require such involvement, its
conviction that American power is no longer a force for
good in the world, and, in general, its relative disinterest
in problems of foreign policy. Moreover, what time itself
may not do, circumstance may instead accomplish.

But even if it is assumed that time and circumstance will
not substantially alter the present outlook of the younger
elite, that Vietnam will remain a "crucial experience" for
this group as Munich was a crucial experience for a preceding generation,** the ultimate effects for American foreign policy remain unclear. It has long been apparent that
the attitudes of college students toward both foreign and
domestic issues are not shared by non-college youth, and
that the differences between young persons on and off
campus are as great as, if not greater than, the differences
between the generations. Nor has the pronounced leftward
movement in campus politics over the course of the war,
and largely as a result of the war, erased the still consider-

---

* See Graham T. Allison, "Cool It: The Foreign Policy of Young
America," *Foreign Policy* (Winter 1970–71), pp. 144–60. Allison's study
concentrates "on a select group of college-educated youth who most
nearly constitute an elite among their contemporaries, in the sense
that they are judged to have a five percent statistical chance of future
appointment to a political or executive position in the US government or to a position of comparable influence in the society" (p. 149).

** Graham T. Allison, "Cool It: The Foreign Policy of Young America,"
p. 156.

able differences that persist among college youth.

In addition, despite the hostility toward foreign policy that the Vietnam War has engendered among college students as a whole, with the end of the war, a majority on campus may be expected to revert to a position far less critical of US foreign policy.* This will almost certainly be true of students at the less selective schools (which contain the great majority of college students), and it may be even partially true of those at the higher quality institutions, who initially led the opposition to Vietnam. Should the present hostility continue to characterize the outlook of the relatively small group that in other circumstances could be expected eventually to conduct the nation's foreign policy, the prospect arises that control over affairs of state will gravitate to a new—if less talented—group.

Ultimately, the attitude of the elite young toward foreign policy, assuming it to persist, could have profound consequences. The full impact of this attitude, however, will not be felt for at least a decade. In the meantime, it is the effects of Vietnam on the public generally that are of greater moment.

That Vietnam has affected for the present the public's attitude toward foreign policy is apparent. Nor can this impact be adequately gauged simply by responses to public opinion poll questions designed to test internationalist and

---

* Opposition to the war among college students as a whole, it should be recalled, did not materialize until the early summer of 1968. It was only in June of that year that approximately half of the college students came to view the war as a mistake, a shift roughly comparable to that of the general public, though one markedly higher than that of 21- to 30-year-olds taken as a whole. Even then, opposition to the war on the campus could hardly be termed pervasive. It was only in 1970 that it became so, with the invasion of Cambodia.

isolationist orientations on a generalized basis.* A continued endorsement of the need for America to play an active role in the world need not carry with it an endorsement of the wherewithal to fulfill that role. Public approval of the broad interests of policy—security, peace, etc.—may be attended by public reluctance to support the necessary means of policy, or at least what an administration judges to be the necessary means of policy.

It is no doubt the case that, even in the absence of the Vietnam War, a rising concern over domestic problems, coinciding as it did with the decline of the cold war, would have had its effects on the public's willingness to support the kind and degree of involvement that has been consistently supported since World War II. But there is no question that Vietnam has been critical in bringing about a public outlook on issues of foreign and military policy which, for the time being at any rate, forms a marked contrast to the outlook of earlier years. It is above all Vietnam that explains the reversal of a long pattern of public support for placing the defense requirements of major security policies over domestic welfare needs. Even more clearly, it is

---

* Even in general questions, the impact of Vietnam appears notable. In *Hopes and Fears of the American People*, Albert Cantril and Charles Roll report that 77 percent of the public agree with the statement: "We shouldn't think so much in international terms but concentrate more on our own national problems and building up our strength and prosperity here at home." This figure represents an increase of 22 percent since 1964, when the Institute for International Social Research tested the public's response to the same statement. The 1964 response, along with public reaction to foreign aid and related issues, led Lloyd A. Free and Hadley Cantril to conclude that the outlook of most Americans "seems best described as one of qualified internationalism." Albert H. Cantril and Charles W. Roll, *Hopes and Fears of the American People*, p. 42. Lloyd A. Free and Hadley Cantril, *The Political Beliefs of Americans: A Study of Public Opinion* (New Brunswick, N.J.: Rutgers University Press, 1967), pp. 64 and 77.

Vietnam that has led to the public's present opposition to employing American ground forces in defense of nations— including America's allies—attacked by communist or communist-backed forces.

What is still not clear, however, is the deeper significance of the apparent change in public mood that the Vietnam War has brought about. Does the public's present mood signal the emergence of new and important constraints on foreign policy, constraints that future administrations will ignore only at their peril? Any attempt to answer this question must take into consideration the manner in which public opinion evolved in the course of the war.

To be sure, there is no difficulty in identifying one all-important constraint that Vietnam has underscored. Public support of foreign policy generally, and military interventions particularly, is conditioned by considerations of cost and effectiveness. But this condition, or constraint, is hardly novel. One observer, assessing the relationship that has developed since World War II between public opinion and foreign policy, concludes: "The public has supported American foreign policy . . . as long as it appeared to be yielding tangible results, or, in the absence of such results, did not impose what the electorate regarded as burdensome costs. When these conditions were not met, a serious erosion in public support began to appear." *

The results of a decade of opinion surveys on the Vietnam War bear out this view. So long as the costs of American involvement in Vietnam were modest, that is, until 1965, the public's attitude was largely one of indifferent support. Successive administrations had defined as a vital

---

* Francis E. Rourke, "The Domestic Scene" in *America and the World: From the Truman Doctrine to Vietnam*, by Robert E. Osgood et al. (Baltimore: The Johns Hopkins Press, 1970), p. 149.

American interest the preservation of a non-communist South Vietnam. The public accepted that definition as it accepted the modest costs of an involvement that, almost from the outset, it did not expect to issue in military victory. During the critical years 1966–67, a majority of the public, despite a growing frustration over the lack of progress in Vietnam, continued to support the war and even to favor the escalation of attacks against North Vietnam. The decisive shift in public opinion, reflected primarily by the conviction that it was a mistake to have intervened in Vietnam, came only in 1968, when the demands imposed by the war reached an unexpectedly high level while the prospects for achieving military victory seemingly remained as far away as ever.* Even then, it is noteworthy that the public continued to give substantial support to the Vietnam policy of the Johnson administration throughout 1968. And if this remaining support for the war measurably eroded in 1969 with the advent of the Nixon administration, the principal reason can probably be traced to the public's belief that the new administration had decided to disengage from Vietnam.

In the light of these considerations, an indisputable lesson that may be learned from Vietnam is that success is the great solvent of serious public disaffection over foreign policy, and particularly over military intervention. Had

---

* A Michigan Survey Research Center finding in 1968 illustrates the error of identifying as a triumph of the doves the prevalence of the conviction that intervention in Vietnam was a mistake. "[Among] those who viewed the war as a mistake almost as many favored escalation as were for withdrawal! All told . . . a five-to-three majority regretted the original intervention, but at the same time those calling for 'a stronger stand even if it means invading North Vietnam' outnumbered those advocating complete withdrawal by about as large a margin." Philip E. Converse and Howard Schuman, " 'Silent Majorities' and the Vietnam War," *Scientific American*, June 1970, p. 20.

the intervention succeeded by 1967, or even by early 1968, it is reasonable to assume that the disillusionment and recriminations of today would not have arisen. It seems equally reasonable to assume that, had the intervention issued in success, the public's attitude toward the use of American military power abroad would be different from what it is today.

It is of course true that from the start opposition to the war was not based simply upon its cost and seemingly inconclusive character. Indeed, if the cost of the war appeared exorbitant to an ever increasing number, it did so in part because the reasons for which the war allegedly was being fought became increasingly suspect. There is no evidence, however, that for the public at large the growing implausibility of the rationale given for the war was the decisive factor in prompting the conviction of a majority that American involvement in Vietnam had been a mistake. On the contrary, the evidence suggests that a majority of those who finally came to view American involvement as a mistake and to favor withdrawal did so primarily on the pragmatic grounds that we had not won the war and showed little prospect of doing so.

These considerations should give pause to those who would draw far-reaching conclusions about the effects of Vietnam on public opinion. No doubt, the public wants no more Vietnams. But this is less than revealing about the nature of the constraints policy-makers will henceforth ignore at their peril, given the distinctive characteristics of the war in Vietnam.

Of possibly greater significance than the sentiment of no more Vietnams is the present opposition of the public to military intervention generally. There is no way of knowing at this point, however, how stable and persistent this anti-interventionist mood will prove to be. Viewed superficially, the opinion surveys registering the public's present opposition to military intervention do indeed appear as a portentous shift away from the mood that has heretofore characterized the entire post-World War II period. But even when viewed superficially, there are features that must qualify the conclusion that a stable and strong public opposition has now developed to the use of American military power abroad.

Of necessity, the relevant opinion surveys have been undertaken in the period (1969–71) of profound public disillusionment over Vietnam, a fact that cannot but affect the results. Time may deepen this disillusionment. It is possible, though, that time will moderate the public's current anti-interventionist disposition. Much will depend upon how Vietnam is seen in retrospect, and this will depend, in large part, upon the ultimate outcome of the war. Then, too, the questions on intervention are hypothetical, and for this reason alone the results can prove quite misleading. In an actual crisis, one must expect the public to be more supportive of involvement than recent surveys indicate, and particularly if the President were to make a strong case for intervention (as presumably he could do for areas of more traditional interest than Southeast Asia).

Finally, in almost every recent survey on intervention, the issue posed was one of employing American ground forces and not one of employing American military power generally. It does not seem unreasonable to assume that a part of the present opposition to future intervention, above all in Asia, is an opposition to the use of American troops in a costly and inconclusive land war rather than an opposition to intervention itself. If this is true, a strategy that moves toward a substantially greater emphasis on aerial and naval power to back up present commitments may evoke little serious public opposition, short of its being put to the test. And even if put to the test, it may receive public sanction, or toleration, provided the use of ground forces is avoided and, of course, provided the effectiveness of intervention can soon be made apparent.*

More important for understanding the character of the public's opposition to intervention, however, is an assessment of the extent to which present public attitudes toward the future use of American military power abroad are based on a changed perception of America's vital interests in addition to a changed perception of the possible threats to those interests. Does the public's current anti-interventionist mood reflect an awareness, however inarticulate, that the conditions of American security have changed, and considerably so, over the past quarter of a century? If it does, then despite the persistence of a residual anti-communism, we may expect an anti-interventionist disposition to continue and, in time, even to deepen.

Yet there is no reliable way at present of determining the extent to which the emergence of an anti-interventionist

---

* It should also be noted that most recent polls on intervention have simply asked whether the respondent would favor sending American troops to the support of a particular state attacked by communist military forces. If a wider choice of alternatives is given, however, a more qualified and complicated picture emerges. In the polling for *Hopes and Fears of the American People*, respondents were given a choice of sending troops, sending military supplies only, or refusing to get involved at all. The predominant response to sending troops, even to defend our NATO allies, was negative. However, a large percentage was willing to send forms of military aid short of ground troops. It is impossible to estimate accurately how many in the latter group, were an actual crisis to arise, would shift over to the group willing to send ground forces if necessary, but it seems only reasonable to assume that a substantial number would be so willing. Cantril and Roll, *Hopes and Fears of the American People*, pp. 47-50.

disposition among the public at large is rooted in a changed perception of American security rather than simply in a reaction to the frustrations engendered by Vietnam. In the case of some groups—the leadership of the younger generation, for example—a strong anti-interventionist disposition does reflect, among other things, a changed perception of the conditions of American security. If, however, we take what is by far the largest group that came to consider the war a mistake, a group less educated and less affluent than the national average, we must come to a different conclusion. There is little reason to believe that, to the extent that this group is now anti-interventionist in outlook, this outlook is the result of any firmly held views, whether of the war or, more generally, of the changed conditions of the nation's security. The members of this group are generally inattentive to issues of foreign policy and hold opinions that are seldom, if ever, sharply crystallized. As such, they are, and will likely continue to be, acquiescent in, if not supportive of, the foreign policy actions taken by the government.

Of much greater importance is the smaller, though still very substantial, group that forms the bulk of the college-educated population and that throughout the post-World War II period has been strongly supportive of the government in foreign policy. Alumni of the less prestigious smaller colleges and universities have provided the hard core of support for the war in Vietnam.* Though now in-

---

* The Michigan Survey Research Center reports: "Throughout the entire period from 1964 to 1968 alumni of the smaller colleges, although they came to see the war as a mistake, clung to a harder line than even the noncollege population. It is this constituency from smaller colleges more than any other that has served as the backbone of popular support for the war." Converse and Schuman, " 'Silent Majorities' and the Vietnam War," p. 23.

creasingly disillusioned over Vietnam, and though in part translating this disillusionment into a present anti-interventionist outlook, it would be rash to conclude that this critically important group is in the process of substantially altering long-held views about the conditions of American security.

The present negative response of the public to the prospect of future intervention must therefore be viewed with caution. In some measure, this response simply registers an unwillingness even to consider future intervention as long as the war in Vietnam is not resolved. To the degree that this is so, it may be that public attitudes toward the war itself are more indicative of future public constraints on American foreign policy than are present attempts to assess the war's impact.

What appears to impress most observers is the dramatic change that has occurred in public attitudes toward the war since 1965, and particularly since 1968. Given the course of the war and all its attendant consequences, however, what seems at least equally impressive is the fact that, despite everything that has happened, a hard core of at least one quarter of the population persists in the belief that the intervention was not a mistake. If we add this group to those who came to believe the war was a mistake, primarily because of a refusal to take all-out measures in order to win it, we have a combined group that numbers between 40 and 50 percent of the population. When these considerations are taken together with the continued reluctance of a substantial minority of the public to abandon South Vietnam until a settlement can be reached that will ensure that the communists do not get control, the essential ambiguity of the "lesson" the public has learned from Vietnam is apparent.

Perhaps the most that can be said with assurance about the current public mood toward foreign policy in general is that, for the first time since the cold war began, it is deeply ambivalent. The fundamental outlook and motives that have formed the basis of broad public support for American foreign policy since World War II—and which must account for so much of the public's permissiveness in foreign policy—clearly have not disappeared, but their compelling force has just as clearly attenuated. The experience in Vietnam has not created insurmountable obstacles to future interventions, but the experience has created obstacles that did not heretofore exist. Anti-communism, so critical in sustaining public support for foreign policy in the past, has not disappeared, but it no longer provides the support it once did. Quite apart from the recent policy moves of the present administration, which must further dissipate this once central public motivation, the world is such today that it simply no longer arouses in the public the intensity of anti-communist commitment that it once aroused.

The consequence of these developments is a marked public uncertainty over America's proper role and interests in the world. In time this uncertainty could be transformed into a demand for change that might go a considerable way toward realizing presidential fears of a new isolationism. Whether it will do so depends in large measure on whether the elites forming the core of the postwar consensus on foreign policy can be reunited in the aftermath of Vietnam. A continued estrangement of the foreign policy elites, or of a substantial portion of these elites, is bound to have its effects on public opinion. This is so even if we assume, as we must assume, that the President will continue to enjoy the unique advantages in the formulation and execution of foreign policy that are the result of constitutional tradition, the immense resources of the executive branch, and the necessities of the international environment.

What was distinctive about domestic reaction to the war in Vietnam was not its lack of popular support in the later stages of the conflict. A comparison between the Vietnam and Korean wars shows that public weariness and disenchantment with each conflict became equally manifest after a certain point.* Vietnam has been distinctive because of the opposition it aroused among the intellectuals and, particularly, among many who comprised the foreign policy elites. It was the defection of the intellectuals, in general, and of a very substantial part of the foreign policy elites, in particular, that proved to be critical in the case of domestic opposition to Vietnam. A similar defection would prove equally critical in determining the course of American policy in the years ahead.

Thus, we return to the questions posed at the outset of this essay. Are there persuasive reasons for believing that a serious and lasting rupture has occurred within the elites who have formed the core of the foreign policy consensus of the past generation? Has the Establishment, to use the President's term, or a substantial part of the Establishment, really defected in the sense that it no longer accepts the substance of the interests and commitments that have defined American foreign policy in the past and continue to define it today?

As in the case of the general public, any attempt to answer these questions must begin by recalling the manner in which elite opinion evolved in the course of the war.

---

* John E. Mueller, "Trends in Popular Support for the Wars in Korea and Vietnam," *American Political Science Review*, June 1971, pp. 358-75.

And, again as in the case of the general public, when this evolution is considered, the difficulties in concluding that the war has led to a breakdown of the foreign policy consensus are apparent. For it was not only the public that responded to pragmatic considerations in changing its attitude toward the war. So did the greater part of those who comprise the foreign policy elites and who, in the initial stages of the war, supported the intervention or, though entertaining reservations about the wisdom of intervention, fell short of clear opposition or, though unreservedly opposed from the start, saw in the war a misapplication of American power given the unfavorable circumstances in which that power was applied.

In the light of the history of the war, and of the correlation between its costly yet frustrating course and the swelling ranks of critics, it does not seem unreasonable to conclude that the majority of liberal and moderate critics came to oppose the intervention not so much because they did not share the outlook and interests that were bound, sooner or later, to issue in a Vietnam, but because they concluded either that the war could not have a successful outcome or that, whatever the outcome, the costs had become entirely disproportionate to the interests at stake.

To the extent that President Nixon's Establishment is understood as comprising those who have been the architects, administrators, and expositors, official and unofficial, of American foreign policy in years past, of what does the apostasy of most of them consist other than a disagreement with the President over the manner in which American involvement in Vietnam should be ended? To be sure, this disagreement itself has been sharp and serious. But it has been so, in large measure, because it has reflected a conviction on the part of the President's influential and articulate critics that, the longer the war was permitted to drag on, the greater would be its cumulative effects on an already disillusioned and frustrated public. To this extent, disagreement, however bitter, over how and when to end the involvement in Vietnam has not been in itself indicative of any broader disagreement over interests considered vital to the nation. Instead, it has been most clearly indicative of a difference over how a disastrous war should be ended so as to prove least injurious to those greater interests.

The significance of the disaffection Vietnam has led to among the foreign policy elites must of course be assessed in terms broader than the issues directly related to the war. For liberal and moderate criticism of American foreign policy, though largely provoked by the war, has gone well beyond Vietnam. To the extent that it has done so, however, has it broken with the basic conceptions of role and interests that have guided postwar policy and that have formed the basis of the postwar consensus on foreign policy? Clearly, it has broken with the perception of the world that prevailed during—and, for a limited time, even after—the period of the classic cold war. But recognition that the world has changed and that American foreign policy must reflect this change is not only generally acknowledged today; it has become the settled orthodoxy of the present administration.

The "fundamental transition in foreign policy" that President Nixon sees his administration leading the nation through proceeds from the recognition that we are at the end of the postwar era and that, with the passing of this era, "are gone the conditions which have determined the assumptions and practice of United States foreign policy

since 1945." * In its emphasis on the changes that have occurred in the world and on the need for American policy
to adjust to those changes, the various formulations of the
Nixon Doctrine evidently assimilate the conventional
criticism of recent years. In doing so, they also assimilate,
though not without qualification, the conventionally critical view of the diminished threat held out to American
interests by a world that is politically and ideologically
pluralistic.

A changed world not only requires change in the
methods of foreign policy; within limits, it also permits
and even requires a redefinition of interests. In a
pluralistic world, the domino theory must at least be modi-
fied. But so also must the interest one has in each and
every domino. If there is no "test case" for wars of national
liberation, the interest one has in defeating any particular
war of national liberation is likely to change. If the process
of modernization is going to prove very slow, and if its
course cannot be controlled by outsiders, there is no need
to see in it a matter of vital concern. If China is no longer
found capable of or intent upon overturning the Asian
balance of power, the interest in containing China may be
re-interpreted. These are among the commonplaces of the
conventionally critical view that change is required not
only in the methods but in the interests of American
policy. They are also among the recognizable features of
the present administration's foreign policy.

A modest redefinition of interests, largely contingent
upon a cautiously optimistic view of the world in which
these interests must be sought, scarcely adds up to a revolution in American foreign policy. In accepting the princi-

---

* Richard M. Nixon, *U.S. Foreign Policy for the 1970's (II): Building
for Peace* (Washington, DC: Government Printing Office, 1971), p. 12.

pal features of the liberal and moderate critique of American policy that developed in the course of the 1960s, the
Nixon administration has shown no disposition to relinquish the nation's predominant role in the world (an
emphasis on partnership and regionalism notwithstand-
ing), or to alter the essential structure of American interests. But neither has the great majority of those who comprise President Nixon's Establishment.

For both, America continues to have a vital interest in
maintaining a world order in which the nation occupies a
predominant position in the international hierarchy. For
both, America has a vital interest in ensuring that change
is effected only in certain ways and that certain kinds of
change are precluded altogether. Certainly, for both, the
maintenance of a favorable balance of power in Europe and
in Asia continues to be seen as a vital American interest
which, in turn, requires preserving the essential structure
of alliance relationships. This being the case, for both,
some kind of containment policy necessarily follows so
long as the Soviet Union and China are deemed to remain
even potentially expansionist powers.* The differences that
persist today over the proper means of containing the
major communist powers are scarcely of epic proportion.
And the marked de-emphasis of the Nixon administration

---

* The point would hardly be worth emphasis were it not for the fact that
a number of commentators have seen in the latest presidential exposi-
tion of American foreign policy the abandonment of containment. The
relevant passage that has prompted this curious view reads: "Our alliances are no longer addressed primarily to the containment of the Soviet
Union and China behind an American shield. They are, instead, addressed to the creation with those powers of a stable world peace. That
task requires the maintenance of the allied strength of the non-
Communist world." Richard M. Nixon, *U.S. Foreign Policy for the
1970's (III): The Emerging Structure of Peace* (Washington, DC: Government Printing Office, 1972), p. 6.

on the ideological side of containment has, if anything, gone beyond the demands of conventional criticism.

Vietnam and its immediate consequences apart, are there serious differences between the President and the Establishment over the critical issue of military intervention in the Third World? To be sure, the Nixon Doctrine can hardly be construed as the acceptance, in principle, of an anti-interventionist position. Intended as a response to the charge of American "globalism," the Nixon Doctrine disavows a policy of unlimited and indiscriminate commitment to preventing communist expansion. It does not disavow intervention where vital American interests are presumably at stake, even if intervention is in response to what is predominantly an internal revolutionary conflict.

But if the anti-interventionism of the Nixon Doctrine is of modest proportion, and conditioned by the expectation that the prospect of communist expansion in the Third World has markedly declined, substantially the same must be said of the anti-interventionism of conventional critics. The latter also attach to their position the qualification that the nation or region in question not constitute, in itself, a vital interest or that, quite apart from the intrinsic importance of the immediate area, the consequence of abstaining from intervention not prove generally destabilizing. And here, as well, a qualified anti-interventionist position is conditioned by the expectation that the prospect of communist expansion in the Third World has markedly declined.

It does not follow from these considerations that there are no differences between President Nixon and the Establishment. Obviously, there are. (Though one of these differences is not, as conventional criticism would have it, that the Nixon Doctrine has no vision that goes beyond stability. What differentiates the present administration from its predecessors is not its attachment to stability but the candor with which it pursues stability. The charge that the attachment itself is something new borders on pure cant.) The question, however, is whether these differences are of such nature as to justify the conclusion that those who have formed the influential and articulate core of the postwar consensus on foreign policy have now defected, that they and the President entertain broadly disparate views of the nation's role and interests in the world. Thus posed, the answer seems apparent. Although there have indeed been some who have turned their backs on "internationalism," as President Nixon conceives of internationalism, the great majority clearly has not done so. It is not surprising that the charge of neo-isolationism has been seen as gratuitous by those whose chief sin has been to oppose the President over how and when the American involvement in Vietnam should be ended.

At the same time, it is true that a substantial portion of the nation's intellectuals have ranged themselves generally in opposition to American foreign policy. Although the intensity of this opposition may be expected to diminish with the ending of the American involvement in Vietnam—and, indeed, has already begun to diminish—in some measure the opposition will undoubtedly persist into the foreseeable future. The effect it will have on the formulation of the nation's foreign policy is necessarily speculative. Even so, it is difficult to see the significance of this opposition, once moderated by the ending of the war, as more than peripheral.

Although there are some notable exceptions, for the most part the irreconcilables consist of those who have never been deeply concerned with foreign policy. If anything, foreign policy, with its grim and repetitive equations of power, has always repelled them. To the extent that they supported American policy in the years of the cold war, they are now filled with guilt over a commitment that in retrospect is seen as little more than seduction by the state. Vietnam aroused them as no other event could. But, in the absence of a Vietnam, what will sustain them? A much less obtrusive American presence abroad, a much more selective strategy of intervention, a sophisticated mixture of accommodation and coercion, a greater reliance on the efforts of allies, and of course a degree of luck are the obvious ingredients of a policy that might well succeed in muting these voices of disaffection while maintaining the substance of America's global interests and commitments.

If the foregoing analysis is sound, it would be rash to foresee domestic pressures as forcing in the near future far-reaching changes in American foreign policy. Though the mood of the public is clearly ambivalent, the American people show little propensity to impose a massive veto on presidential action in foreign policy, at least so long as this action avoids a repetition of the events associated with Vietnam. In the absence of these events, it also seems likely that the influence of dissentient elites will be minimized.

But even if domestic pressures are contained, the changes that have occurred in the world over the past generation will continue to challenge policies, the rationale of which reflects the world of yesterday more than the world of today. Ultimately, it is the pressures generated by the international environment that may be expected to force a transformation of the American role and interests. Should those pressures push the nation toward a policy of

isolationism that was once presumably abandoned for-
ever (or should national leadership unexpectedly choose to
move toward an isolationist policy), it is only a thralldom
to a misunderstood past that finds in this prospect a threat
rather than a promise.

EPILOGUE

IN THE COURSE OF WRITING THIS ESSAY, I have had occasion to present its central themes to several groups. Invariably, and not unexpectedly, the responses have centered on two major issues: the use of the term isolationism, and the anticipated costs of pursuing a policy—whatever the term one attaches to it—that advocates withdrawal from security commitments made over the past generation. The responses have been illuminating and warrant, by way of conclusion, brief consideration.

It is apparent that the term isolationism continues to provoke an almost instinctively hostile reaction. This is true even for those who otherwise favor a policy that is, in its essential features, indistinguishable from isolationism. In part, this resistance may be attributed simply to a misunderstanding of what isolationism as a policy entails and has always entailed. A policy of isolationism is still found by many to imply the absence of all significant relationships between America and the other nations of the world rather than the absence of certain relationships. It is this misunderstanding that often explains the curious insistence of those who favor an isolationist policy today that they are not isolationists. They are like the man who has been speaking prose all his life but has yet to become aware of this fact.

In part, resistance to the term isolationism may also be traced to the conviction that one must either pursue a policy of isolationism everywhere or refrain from pursuing it anywhere. In this view, isolationism is like pregnancy. A little of either is impossible. In America's case alone, however, the historical record clearly refutes this view, since we were isolationist with respect to the world at large at the same time that we were interventionist with respect to the Caribbean and Central America. The fact that we were interventionist in this hemisphere did not prevent us from being isolationist outside the hemisphere. Nor has it precluded the conventionally accepted designation of a policy as isolationist that, in fact, was not "pure" isolationism. There is no apparent reason then for rejecting the term isolationism as applied to a future policy that might once again limit military intervention to this hemisphere. For that matter, there is no apparent reason for rejecting the term isolationism as applied to a policy that firmly eschews alliances and military intervention save in the case of Western Europe. To be sure, the latter policy would scarcely be isolationist by interwar standards. But by the standards of the postwar period it plainly would be so.

Perhaps the most pervasive objection to the term isolationism must be attributed simply to the negative reaction it regularly evokes. Given this reaction, the argument has been urged by many otherwise sympathetic to an isolationist policy that the term is beyond rehabilitation and that another term be used in advocating what is in effect a new isolationism. (It is partly for this reason that a new isolationism not infrequently appears today in the guise of a new internationalism.) In view of the misunderstanding and misuse that have marked the dread epithet, there is a good deal to be said for this argument. The difficulty, however, is that the term cannot be exorcised so simply. Quite apart from its continued utility in the political marketplace, it denotes an historical experience that is of enduring significance. Moreover, it expresses an element of the American outlook and psyche that is not ephemeral. Rather than to accept the argument that isolationism must remain a millstone around the neck of anyone unfortunate enough to be tagged with it, the sensible course would seem that of rehabilitating a badly abused term. Whether isolationism is rejected or accepted, it ought at least to be seen for what it is and its disadvantages or advantages examined soberly.

It hardly needs emphasizing that we cannot know all of the disadvantages and advantages of pursuing an isolationist policy. At best, we can only make an educated guess at the consequences, always bearing in mind the probable environment in which an isolationist policy would be pursued. Despite an occasional lapse, we have acknowledged not only that the costs of isolationism remain partly indeterminate but that there will be costs. Many have taken this acknowledgment as a peculiar weakness of the argument. It is so, however, only if the absurd assumption is made either that present policies entail no costs or that such costs as they do entail are calculable. That men should prefer the known to the unknown is only reasonable, provided of course that the known does not appear too intolerable. Even so, they ought not to equate what they are doing with the known, in the sense that the consequences of what they are doing are assumed to be determinate. The experience of the past decade surely affords a dramatic refutation of this assumption.

The experience of the past decade also affords a dramatic refutation of the penchant for rejecting novel courses of action simply because they are novel. Although the habit of dismissing the unconventional as unthinkable persists, what is noteworthy are the recent occasions in which heresy has been suddenly transformed into orthodoxy. Thus, a view of the Third World that was dismissed as merely eccentric in the early 1960s became the conventional wisdom of the late 1960s. So, too, international monetary arrangements that were deemed impossible in the late 1960s became inevitable in the early 1970s. Given this experience, one is at least entitled to ask that the case for a new isolationism be given serious consideration rather than being simply dismissed out of hand.

It is apparent that many people still have considerable difficulty in coming to terms with the changed structure of the American security position. The hold that the past continues to exercise over the present is so strong that nuclear-missile weapons are still not commonly seen to invalidate conventional balance-of-power considerations. Thus, the statement that control of Western Europe by a hostile power would not substantially alter the threat to America's physical security continues to provoke strong opposition. Yet the fact remains that a Soviet Union in control of Western Europe would be no less vulnerable to destruction by American strategic power than it is today. Nor would America be more vulnerable to destruction by Soviet strategic power than it is today. The point cannot be made too often that to the extent security is equated with physical security, conventional balance-of-power calculations have become irrelevant—or very nearly so—for the great nuclear states.

Even when this point is accepted, however, objection

is often taken to the position that America's core security would not be jeopardized by the proliferation of nuclear weapons we assume would attend a general American withdrawal. (The likelihood of proliferation is itself challenged by some who argue it is not at all clear that this would be one of the consequences of an American withdrawal. Although we may have too readily accepted the assumption that proliferation would attend withdrawal, it does not seem unreasonable to assume that an isolationist America would create a strong disposition on the part of at least some states to acquire nuclear weapons.) There is no gainsaying the argument that, all other things being equal, the greater the number of states possessing nuclear weapons the greater the chances of a nuclear conflict. States that do not have nuclear weapons evidently cannot be tempted to use them. The relevant question, however, is not whether nuclear proliferation increases the chances of nuclear conflict, but whether this increase is such as to have any practical significance.

If, for example, we assume that an American withdrawal would prompt Japan to acquire nuclear weapons and lead the Western Europeans to develop an effective nuclear capability, would this significantly increase the prospects of a nuclear conflict? It would not seem so, unless we further assume that the major states we have long been allied to are less prudent, or less virtuous, than the states we have long looked upon as our great adversaries.

It is of course another matter to consider the prospects of nuclear conflict in a world where a substantial number of states possess nuclear forces (however small and ineffective these forces may be in relation to the nuclear forces of the great states). Even in today's world, one may still question whether the prospects of nuclear conflict would significantly increase. Our point, though, is not to dispute that they would significantly increase but to ask why this prospect should be seen as a threat to America's physical security. It will not do to answer this question on the basis of America's present interests and commitments in the world, for we are postulating a radical change in the nation's interests and commitments. Clearly, if the nation's vital interests continue to be equated with the maintenance of global stability and order, an increased prospect of nuclear conflicts must also increase the chances of American involvement in such conflicts. Once this equation and the commitments it has led to are abandoned, however, the consequences of proliferation to America's physical security also change.

If these considerations are nevertheless viewed with skepticism even by many who otherwise favor substantial change in the nation's foreign policy, the principal reason seems to be the deep and persistent fear that a nuclear peace is somehow indivisible. It is this fear that is at the root of the question frequently put today: What would have happened in the recent conflict between India and Pakistan if the contestants had possessed nuclear weapons and had given way to the temptation to use them? Yet apart from immeasurably worsening an already tragic situation, one response seems clear. The disposition of an American government to become involved would have been no greater than it proved to be in the actual case.

In dealing with the costs of adopting an isolationist policy, I have emphasized the reduction of American influence consequent upon a withdrawal from present commitments. No one can say with any assurance how great this loss would be. What does seem clear is that American influence in the world would be substantially reduced. It is significant that this prospect is nevertheless viewed with apprehension and opposition by many who supposedly desire the end of American predominance. How one can will the end of American predominance without also willing the reduction of American influence remains no less obscure than how one can will the goal of a devolution of power without also willing the means—nuclear proliferation—indispensable to this goal. What are we to conclude about those who pose as critics of American foreign policy, and who insist upon basic changes in policy, yet who shrink from prospects—reduced American influence, nuclear proliferation, a greater measure of instability, etc.— that are the inevitable concomitants of such change? The suspicion persists that the great majority of ostensible critics of American foreign policy are critical of a style or outlook rather than of policy itself and that, to the extent that they have a substantive disagreement with this and preceding administrations, it is principally one that concerns the methods rather than the interests of policy.

On occasion, the view has been taken that even if an American withdrawal would result in the reduction of American influence, it would not of necessity result in the increase of Soviet (or Chinese) influence. In the case of Western Europe, in particular, skepticism has been voiced over the assertion that an American withdrawal, even in quite favorable circumstances, can be expected to result in a substantial increase of Russian influence. How, it is asked, would this increase of Russian influence in European affairs be manifested? It seems unnecessary to attempt a detailed reply to this question. If we assume, as I do, that, despite a growing separation between military power and political influence, an important relationship between power and influence nevertheless persists, the general response is apparent. To insist upon delineating the precise manifestations this increased Soviet influence would take, before acknowledging the prospect of increased influence at all, appears obtuse.

It is another matter, however, to question the assertion that an American withdrawal from Europe would result in turning the continent into a huge Finland. Why should the three major states of Western Europe, possessing in common as they do two-thirds of the population and economic power of the Soviet Union, submit to this fate? For, unlike Finland, only through a deliberate act of submission on the part of the three major states of Western Europe could the Soviet Union come to exercise anything like a comparable degree of influence over Western European affairs. True enough, it is often the Europeans themselves who project this consequence of an American withdrawal even while complaining of America's hegemonic role in Europe's defense (and even while doubting that any American government would in fact risk America's cities in the defense of Europe). There is no reason to doubt that those who may resent America's continued military hegemony may also be deeply apprehensive over the prospect that the American protectorate will one day come to an end. One is reminded of the child who rebels at its dependence, yet is fearful of assuming its independence. In the case of Europe, however, the "child" has the resources and certainly the maturity to assume—or, rather, resume—its full independence. Given only a sufficient will to do so, and a moderate amount of assistance and encouragement by the American "parent," there is little reason to fear that the still proud and great states of Western Europe would be reduced to the status of Finland.

The argument has been put forth that, even if a new

isolationism is possible, it would necessitate a substantial increase in military expenditures. Why should isolationism have this result, however, unless it is assumed that America's security is still determined by conventional balance-of-power calculations? Once this assumption is discarded, as it must be discarded, the argument that isolationism would require a larger defense budget loses its plausibility. At most, the strategic and conventional naval forces required by the new policy would be no greater than the strategic and conventional naval forces required by the present policy. To be sure, it may be contended that the size and quality of these forces must in any event be determined by the size and quality of similar forces maintained by the Soviet Union. But, even if this contention is accepted without question, it has no particular bearing on the military establishment required by an isolationist America. It is presumably applicable whatever policy the nation pursues. The vision of an isolationist America as a beleaguered fortress, required to expend an ever increasing amount for defense, recalls the world of the 1930s and 1940s. Not only is this vision largely irrelevant today, but it has also been largely irrelevant for some time. Rather than necessitate a larger defense budget, the forces projected for an isolationist policy may be expected to result in a modest—though still significant—decline in military expenditures as compared to the expenditures required by present policies.

Although the case against isolationism is almost always argued in terms of the nation's security and well-being, there is no intrinsic reason why it cannot go beyond an argument that centers on the nation's self-interest. Indeed, it is apparent that part of the opposition to isolationism is based on an implicit idealism and not only on an explicit realism. Isolationism is opposed, among other reasons, because it is equated with indifference to the fate of others. Is this equation justified? In large measure, it undoubtedly is, and no useful purpose is served by evasiveness on this point.

In theory, an isolationist America need not be an America indifferent to the fate of others. In practice, however, it is very likely to be much less concerned with its external environment, at least to the extent that concern is measured primarily by deed rather than by word. (In word and sentiment, of course, we have always manifested a concern over, and even acknowledged a duty in, bringing the blessings of freedom to all men through the power of our example. Isolationism and the mission of regenerating the world have only seldom been seen as contradictory.) The seriousness of a nation's concern with the fate of others is normally proportionate to the strength of the conviction that its fate is tied to a common fate. An isolationist America, no longer prompted to define its interests as it has defined them in the recent past, would be a more indifferent America.

At the same time, the equation of isolationism and indifference may be, and often is, pushed too far. If we are right in arguing that a new isolationism would not significantly affect our economic involvement abroad, there is little reason to assume that isolationism would lead us to the kind of indifference that would jeopardize this involvement. Thus, an America that no longer assumed its fate to be inextricably tied to the fate of the developing states would still have an interest in the latter if only by virtue of its continuing economic involvement. It is evidently the case that this involvement cannot be expected to evoke the intensity of concern evoked by the vision of a common fate. Even so, it can be expected to prevent us from simply disinteresting ourselves in the prospect of the impoverished remaining impoverished. There are, after all, other developed states that devote a proportionately comparable portion of their wealth to the Third World, yet who do so without evoking the vision of a common fate we have insisted upon in the recent past.

Moreover, when considering the perils of indifference, we ought not to neglect the perils of concern. If our experience of the past decade has taught us anything, it is the lesson that the consequences of the latter are no less to be guarded against than of the former. It is true that the identification of the collective self with something larger than the self has been a principal source of what justice men have been capable of showing in their collective relations. In a world marked by great disparities of power, this identification, which is the tap root of concern, has nevertheless been at least as productive of injustice among states as of indifference. It is only a naive reading of the history of state relations that neglects these altogether commonplace considerations and insists upon condemning isolationism for its apparent indifference.

DATE DUE

NOV 18 1985			
30 505 JOSTEN'S			